Reach Out—Touch Him

"If only I may touch His garment, I shall be made well."

—Matthew 9:21

Daniel S. Gordeuk, MD

Copyright © 2012 by Diane Gordeuk.
All rights reserved.

All references to Scripture are from The Nelson Study Bible, New King James Version, Thomas Nelson Publishers, Inc., Nashville, ©1997; New King James Version, copyright ©1979, 1980, 1982 by Thomas Nelson, Inc.

Back cover photo by Dick Brown. Interior photos by Diane J. Gordeuk.

ISBN: 1478227044
ISBN-13: 9781478227045

*To Diane and David, whose faith
was a shining standard through my time of trouble*

CONTENTS

Preface xi

Prologue xiii

1. Misha's Story, the Beginning of Mine 1
2. Dan Gordeuk, MD, on Call 5
3. Role Reversal—Diagnosis: Terminal 9
4. The Prayer of Healing 13
5. The Crusade 19
6. Struggles with Belief and Doubt 23
7. Understanding God's Love and Provision for Healing 29
8. Confounding the Doctors: Wellness and Strength Return . . . 35
9. God's Call 39
10. The Holy Spirit Speaks to Me 51
11. Testament 57
12. Overcoming 61
13. Healing the Sick and Dying 65
14. Steps to Belief, Healing and Maintenance 71
15. Retrospection 77

16. Diane's Perspective 81

Epilogue: Medicines, Medical Treatment, and Healing
without Use of Them................................. 89

Afterword 91

Acknowledgments 93

End Notes... 95

PREFACE

As I was writing *Reach Out—Touch Him,* tears of praise and gratitude to God fell on its pages. The story of His healing of my advanced, terminal prostate cancer is a testimony to the awesome power of the Living God, Whom I love and serve. God's declaration in His Word, "I am the Lord, I do not change,"[1] shouts to the reader from the pages of this book. It is my intention that Jesus be lifted up and the power of the Holy Spirit be seen by anyone who reads this account.

Daniel S. Gordeuk, M.D.

PROLOGUE

Dim light shone on the X-ray stretcher where I lay. Diane and two-year-old David stood beside me. Being a general surgeon, I knew the look on the doctor's face only too well.

He spoke my name gently and delivered the diagnosis hesitantly, even timidly. But to me, the words came like thunder: "Dan…there's bad news. You have prostate cancer."

If I had been an elderly man, a modicum of medication might have controlled my condition until some other illness eventually took my life. But I was forty-nine, and in a middle-aged man such as I, prostate cancer is virulent and extremely aggressive. I managed to voice my worst fear, and the doctor confirmed it: the cancer had spread into my bones, had metastasized to every part of my body but my hands, forearms and feet.

"Doctor," I said with effort, "there's no cure, is there?"

"No, there is no cure, Dan," he said.

I was dying. As I lay there, my thoughts flashed back to the day when, as a boy of six, I had accepted Jesus as my Savior. I had wondered, more than once since then, *Will the reality of Jesus be with me when I'm dying?*

Now, the time had come for me to find out.

✤ ✤ ✤

CHAPTER 1

MISHA'S STORY, THE BEGINNING OF MINE

*For God so loved the world that He gave His only begotten Son,
that whoever believes in Him should not perish
but have everlasting life. –John 3:16*

Six years old—I was the same age as the boy in the story when my mother first told me about him. I was a middle-class American child, but the boy, Misha, was born in northern Russia, into a home of privilege. His parents, General Ivan Ivanoff and his wife, Julia, somehow knew that in their son, Misha, their wealth had increased out of proportion to all their earthly possessions. He was the pride of their family, the joy of their lives; nothing was too good for the boy. But in this remote country of firs and white birches where Misha lived, there were no schools. Accordingly, the general sent off to Germany for a tutor for Misha.

The tutor came and set up a schoolroom for the boy on his parents' estate, and soon Ivan and Julia could see that their son was a good student; he learned very quickly. There was one thing, though, that Misha's parents had not expected. The boy's teacher knew Jesus as his Savior. He served the living God and, as he told Misha, Jesus was his best friend.

Reach Out—Touch Him

As Misha's respect for his tutor grew day by day, a close bond developed between the two. One day, Misha asked his teacher if he could also have Jesus as his best friend. Quietly the boy and the man knelt at Misha's wooden desk, and Misha asked Jesus Christ to forgive him of his sins, cleanse his heart, and give him God's gift of eternal life. Tears of earnestness, then of happiness, fell from the faces of the little boy and his teacher onto the schoolroom floor.

Misha jumped up and went running to tell his papa about his newfound friend. His words were full of eagerness. "Papa, I have a new friend, my best friend, and He has changed me into a new boy!"

The general looked at his young son, so full of joy and enthusiasm. He did not have the heart to tell Misha there was no God, no Jesus. As Misha skipped happily back to his classroom, the general turned to his wife and said, "Julia, this is just a passing childhood fancy. Let's let him have his fun, his new friend. He will soon forget about Jesus."

In the days and weeks that followed, the Ivanoffs were surprised to see that their son didn't forget his friend Jesus. He seemed to talk about Him every day, and somehow, Misha really did seem different. He was exceptionally obedient, always said he was sorry when he had done wrong, and read his Bible every day.

One morning when it was time for Misha to come down to breakfast, he told his mother he didn't feel well. "I don't think I can get up for school," he added softly.

Later in the morning, Misha still lay in bed. He didn't want to play and scarcely touched the lunch that Julia brought for him on a tray.

The next day, the boy was no better. With growing concern, Julia sent for a physician, who arrived the following day. After a week of examining and trying to help Misha, the doctor called the Ivanoffs to their son's room. Outside the door he gave them the sad news. "Misha has a rare blood disease which has no cure. I cannot help him. He's going to die."

Misha's Story, the Beginning of Mine

Barely holding back their tears, Misha's father and mother tiptoed into his room. There he lay, so pale, so weak. The little boy must have sensed what the doctor had confided. He said, "Mama, Papa, I'm going to go to be with my friend Jesus soon. Don't cry. I'll be happy with Jesus, and He loves me. Please promise me that when I die, you'll take Jesus as your best friend, too, so we can all be together in heaven someday."

What could the broken-hearted parents do? They looked solemnly into their little son's face and promised him that they would come to know Jesus as their best friend.

Soon, Misha died. When his funeral was over and the guests had left the cemetery, Ivan and Julia stood beside his small grave, feeling as if their hearts would break into a thousand pieces. Looking across the freshly mounded soil at his wife, the general said, "Julia, do you remember what we promised Misha?"

"Yes," she murmured, tears streaming down her face.

The two knelt together, and the general prayed to his son's friend, "Jesus, if you are there, hear our prayer. Forgive us of our sins. Be our best friend as you were little Misha's, and we will serve You."

"Amen," whispered Julia.

They stood to their feet and embraced as if they would never stop, for they both realized that a miracle had occurred. God had made Himself real to them, and they would never be the same. Their tears of sorrow had turned to tears of joy and hope.

As they kept the promise they had made to Misha, they also kept the promise they made that day to Jesus. They served Him the rest of their days and became a strong influence for Jesus Christ in that part of Russia. They were lights in a darkened land, lifting up Jesus, who would draw all people to Himself.[1]

Reach Out—Touch Him

My mother, who told this story to me, was born into a Christian home in Russia. In her village of Suloyiha, 200 miles northwest of Moscow, she heard of the general and his wife who had been led to Jesus by their dying little son. She came to the United States as a fourteen-year-old girl and, seventeen years later, married Stephen Gordeuk, Jr., VMD, a professor at the Pennsylvania State University. My parents started a Christian home, and I was the first of six children.

When I first heard my mother tell of Misha and his parents, I thought, *Little boys get sick, and little boys die sometimes. Misha got sick, and he died.* In my little mind, I thought of dying, like Misha, and I wanted Jesus to be my best friend.

"Dad...Mom, I don't think I know Jesus as my best friend," I confided. "Could you pray for me?" My parents led me into the bedroom, where we knelt by the bed. Like Misha, I prayed for forgiveness of my sins and accepted God's gift of eternal life.[2] I promised to serve Jesus.

❖ ❖ ❖

CHAPTER 2

DAN GORDEUK, MD, ON CALL

*In all your ways acknowledge Him,
and He shall direct your paths.*
—*Proverbs 3:6*

The phone is ringing next to my pillow. As I reach for it, immediately alert, a glance at my watch tells me it's 2:53 AM.

"Dr. Gordeuk?" asks a strained voice from the ER (emergency room at the hospital).

"Yes," I reply quietly.

"I have a twenty-four-year-old white male who was in an MVI (motor vehicle accident). His blood pressure has dropped to 70 palpable, and it has not come up after three liters of fluid IV (intravenous drip). His abdomen is rigid."

"Have you typed and crossed him for four units of packed red blood cells?" I ask.

"Six units," the ER doctor answers tensely.

"Call the OR (operating room) crew immediately, and make sure you have two large IVs going—a 16- or 14-gauge line, if possible. I'll be there in seven minutes."

I'm already pulling on my jeans and reaching for a shirt as I replace the receiver in its cradle.

Reach Out—Touch Him

I run down the stairs on tiptoe, trying not to wake my wife, Diane, who is pregnant with our first child. The moon that was shining brightly when I went to sleep is no longer visible as I step from the porch. Instead, there is snow falling lightly, softly. Seeing it already accumulating on the edges of our lane, I understand how the boy might have gotten into an accident. *So, it will take me nine minutes instead of seven*, I calculate as I pull on the four-wheel drive lever in the Suburban.

I scarcely glance at the receptionist as I walk through the ER's automatic doors; the ER doc is holding an X-ray in front of himself, waving it at me. "Two fractured ribs," he states succinctly, "eleventh and twelfth on left."

"Fractured spleen, likely," I reply, more to myself than to him.

Examining the patient, I look down at his pale, gray face. A blond, blue-eyed youth.

"Oh God, doctor, am I going to make it?" he asks, teeth chattering.

"We'll ask God to help us with the surgery. You'll be okay," I answer quietly. "Is your family here?"

"Not yet," whispers the nurse beside me.

"We'll be operating on you in a few minutes," I explain to the boy. His eyes are closed now; he nods his head.

"Write up a verbal permission for the OR," I tell the nurse. "I'll sign it."

A minute later, I run down the hall to the OR suite, unbuttoning my shirt. Sticking my head around the corner, I shout at the blue-clad, masked nurses, "Fractured spleen, probably—young guy. Send for two units of packed cells now and have them in the OR."

I get rid of my shirt and pull on a pair of green scrub pants. "No shirts," I say aloud to myself as I search through the bin. *Oh well*, I think, putting on a mask and hat. I run down the hall with no shirt—green or otherwise—and start to scrub at the sink in the OR as the patient is being anesthetized.

"Going swimming?" asks a nurse.

"No shirts in the bin," I tell her. I notice stares from the scrub nurse and nurse anesthetist as I hold out my arms for the gown. "No shirts," I explain.

As it turns out, it *is* the spleen, fractured beyond repair. We remove it quickly and find no other intra-abdominal injuries.

"I think we can get by without giving him any blood," I tell the anesthesia doctor at the head of the OR table. He and the nurse anesthetist are absorbed in their work.

"Spleen out already?" he asks, glancing up.

"Yes. I told the boy we'd ask God to help us, and He has."

"Yeah," says the doc, with no evident feeling.

As I leave the OR suite wearing blue jeans and my own shirt, I see the parents of the boy stand up before the doors are fully open. "Is Devin okay?" they chorus.

"Yes," I answer. "He had a fractured spleen, which we removed. He also has two fractured ribs. All he has to do now is to heal. We can trust the Lord for that."

"Thank you," they both say as they sink back into the OR lounge chairs. Their relief is obvious.

My watch shows that it's 4:56 AM as I walk through the snow, now three inches deep, climb into my Suburban and head home.

"Is he okay?" Diane asks sleepily as I slip into bed for an hour's more sleep.

"Yes. Fractured spleen—auto accident." My voice trails off and I'm asleep before I can say more.

An hour later I'm up, getting ready for 7:00 AM hospital rounds, which precede OR schedule time at 7:45.

✠ ✠ ✠

CHAPTER 3

ROLE REVERSAL—DIAGNOSIS: TERMINAL

...and to him the Lord said in a vision, "Ananias."
And he said, "Here I am, Lord."
—Acts 9: 10b

This year had been a busy one. While running for the U. S. House of Representatives in the Fifth District of Pennsylvania, I had spent six to eight hours a day by the phone, and it seemed that this activity was causing the sciatic pain in my right hip and leg to worsen. I had noticed some sciatic pain such as this at various times over the past four years, and now, in December, it was becoming really troublesome. At times I had pain in the left hip and even in my lower ribs in the back. The orthopedic surgeon caring for me prescribed Oxycodone.[1] I was on twelve pills a day, and I still could not sleep at night. This was my weekend on call, but I had to ask my partner to fill in for me because my back pain was too severe for me to operate.

"Hey, Dan," my younger brother offered, "maybe there's something else wrong with you." Victor is a professor of medicine in the field of oncology and hematology.

"What should I do, Vic?" I asked.

Reach Out—Touch Him

"Let's go to the ER and have an internal medicine doctor meet us there and check you."

"All right," I said in a tone of resignation.

Vic drove Diane and me, along with our son David, then two-and-a-half years old, to the emergency room. The doctor examined me and ordered blood tests, a bone scan, and a CT scan of the abdomen and pelvis.

As I lay on the stretcher in the X-ray department with Diane and little David beside me, the doctor came into the room to tell me what he had discovered. He looked uncomfortable.

"Dan…there's bad news. You have prostate cancer." The words were spoken quietly, but their meaning had the effect of thunder.

"Is it metastatic[2]?" I asked with alarm.

"Yes, I'm afraid it is."

"Doctor…there is no cure, is there?" I knew the answer but asked anyway.

"No, there is no cure, Dan."

He went on to tell me that my PSA[3] was 1,300. A normal reading is anywhere from zero to four, and I had never heard of one so high. The bone scan showed cancer in all the bones except the hands, forearms and feet. The CT scan showed a huge prostate tumor, confirmed by the physical exam[4] to be fist-sized. I was anemic[5] and had lost thirteen pounds.

As a surgeon, I knew that a man forty-nine years old with metastatic prostate cancer, and with so much tumor growing in his bone marrow that red blood cell production was decreased,[6] was going to die. Whereas, in an elderly man, prostate cancer is relatively easy to coax into long-term remission, there was no surgery, medicine, or radiological treatment that could cure this tumor in a man my age.

It was at this instant that something miraculous occurred. I had wondered throughout my life whether my faith in Jesus Christ would be real when death was imminent. Now, I knew I was dying. Diane and David were close to my stretcher; the doctor and my oncologist brother were a step behind them. At once, the room was filled with a glorious presence that was undeniable and marvelous. Diane, David, my brother Vic, and the attending doctor looked to me like tiny figures. Never in my life had I known God's presence in such a real and powerful way. The room seemed filled with light, and in the midst of it, I had a vision.[7] I could see myself lying in human hands. Then I could see myself held instead in God's hands. I grasped the message: *In human hands my case was hopeless, but in God's hands, it was one-hundred percent curable.*

The doctor tried to admit me to the hospital, but I wanted to be at home with my family. Later, I learned that the doctor was afraid I might commit suicide because of the devastating news he had given me.

Lying in each other's arms at home that night, Diane and I cried and cried.

"Dan," Diane whispered, "God spared your life when you were before a firing squad in Africa. He spared you, on an icy, crumbling cliff in Colorado, from falling to the rocks below. He has spared you several other times. And now, I don't know how He's going to do it, but He will bring you through this, too." She was referring in the first instance to the time when I'd taken emergency call for a missionary surgeon in South Africa, then visited Mt. Kilimanjaro. From there, I rode to Nairobi, Kenya, on a mini-bus excursion and found myself (and the Scandinavian teachers on board with me) in the midst of a military coup, facing the rifles of nervous guerrillas who had lined us up against a wall. I prayed what I thought would be my last prayer, and then the commander changed his mind, ordered us back into the bus, and told us to "get out of here."

The second incident occurred on the William's Peak range in Colorado as my brother Dave and I, along with our friend Scott, tried to spot an elk herd we had seen from below. My wife was right—I

Reach Out—Touch Him

had come close to death on these and a couple of other occasions in my life. Each time, I had prayed, and each time, God had spared my life. Diane was sure He'd do it again.

This was the moment when I realized the monumental faith in God that Diane had. And yet I thought, *She says this, but she's not a doctor. She doesn't know how hopeless this is.* Immediately, the vision came flooding back, along with the thought, *In human hands my case is hopeless, but in God's hands, it is one-hundred percent curable.*

As we fell asleep, we had no idea what miracles were about to happen.

❋ ❋ ❋

CHAPTER 4

THE PRAYER OF HEALING

"And whatever things you ask in prayer, believing, you will receive."
—Matthew 21: 22

Early the next morning, we were awakened by the ringing of the phone. Diane answered it then turned to me. "It's your partner, Dan. He says, don't worry about anything; he'll take call. Take as long as you need to get well. Is there anything he can do?"

This was the first of forty phone calls that day. By noon, Diane had put a pillow over the kitchen phone and unplugged all the others, letting the answering machine take over.

Later, I phoned my father. "Dad, I'm sick," I said, barely keeping my voice steady. "The doctors say I'm going to die."

My father's voice was strong. "Dan, I was praying for you at 3:00AM. I prayed, 'Lord, if it's Your will, heal my son…' The Lord said, 'Stop. Don't pray like that. It *is* My will.' So, I prayed, 'Lord, heal Dan one-hundred percent.' …Son, the Lord gave me the knowledge that He is going to heal you."

Four other times in my life, I had heard my dad say the Lord had spoken to him. On each of these occasions, the events that followed proved his spiritual insight. It was great encouragement to me to hear his words now.

Then, too, from the outset my wife, Diane, talked of little else than God's power to heal me. She reminded me now of what she'd said last night, of the time in Africa when I was ordered to stand in front of a stone wall, hands up. The fatigue-clad guerrillas pointed semi-automatic weapons at me while deciding whether or not to kill me. "God spared your life!" Diane told me. She brought again to my remembrance, as well, the day an icy, rocky cliff crumbled beneath me on a Colorado mountainside and I could have fallen to the rocks below. "God spared you!" she repeated. She spoke with conviction of the time when my open boat was filling with water twenty miles from shore on the icy Alaskan waters near Kodiak and I was able to start the second outboard engine and bail out enough water to make it to shore. "God spared your life," Diane said once more. "God did not give you a son, who needs a dad, only to let you die and not be there to raise him." Her eyes were filled with tears, but she spoke with certainty. "God heals people, Dan."

When my family takes a trip, we study the brochures. We research the climate, the hotels, and what kinds of things there are to do in the area we plan to visit. Should we take heavy clothes or tee shirts? Will we be able to swim or fish or ski at the places we're considering? These are questions we need to answer before we set out.

Because my cancer had already advanced to the terminal stage I realized that, short of a miracle, it would continue to take its natural course, and soon I would go on a trip. I would leave this world and go to an eternal home—but I had not studied well enough the information in the brochure, the Word of God. I was not intimately familiar with what it would be like in heaven and what God had planned

The Prayer of Healing

for me. Nor was I well acquainted with His promise regarding physical healing. I had not heard from the Lord through His Word on a regular basis. The result of my thoughts about all of this was a feeling of panic. I began to read the Bible with all the energy I could muster.

The same day my father had spoken with me about his prayer for me, my brother Dave called me. Dave, a pastor in Kansas, had been talking to Vic, my physician brother, and realized how sick I was.

"I was driving to work today, crying and thinking of your being sick," Dave told me. "I prayed, 'Lord, give me a verse for my big brother.' I opened my Bible on the seat beside me, and my eyes fell on this verse: Psalm 50:15." I heard Dave's voice reclaim a cheerful tone as he quoted, "'Call upon Me in the day of trouble, and I will deliver you, and you shall glorify Me.'"

"Time for lunch." Diane told me from the doorway of our bedroom. "Are you coming?"

I wasn't hungry. My pajamas hung loosely on me because of my recent weight loss. I responded, not to my stomach's call, but to my family's, "I'll be there in a few minutes."

I inched my way out of bed—a process which now took me four or five minutes—put on my bathrobe and went to lunch. As I joined Diane and David at the table, I knelt on one knee and then half sat on a chair, half kneeled, as I had done now for several weeks. It was too painful to sit upright.

"Diane, you pray," I said.

"I'll pray, Daddy," David proffered. "Dear God, thank you for our food. Make Daddy better. Jesus' name. Amen."

Prayer. In the next ten days, more than thirty people either wrote, phoned or spoke to me in person, all telling me the same

Reach Out—Touch Him

things, almost in the same words: "While we were praying for you—and this has never happened to us before—God told us He was going to heal you." This message came from people in geographic locations ranging from Florida to Pennsylvania and as far west as Indiana. These people did not know one another. That the same words came from so many unrelated people from so many places could not be a coincidence.

Two days after my diagnosis was established, I received a letter from a nurse whom I had not seen since my surgical training. She wrote, "I was praying for you, and God gave me this verse—it's for you! 'And whatever things you ask in prayer, believing, you shall receive.' Matthew 21:22." I marked the verse in my Bible with a yellow highlighter and prayed, pointing to it, perhaps ten times a day, "Lord, You said this; I didn't say this. I believe You."

That same day, a pastor from a nearby church came to our door. "Doctor Gordeuk?" he asked when I opened the door. "The Lord impressed upon me that I should stop and tell you that He wants to heal you." He explained that he had driven past our lane three times, debating whether or not to approach the house, and had almost decided to leave, when the Lord impressed clearly upon him the need to stop and deliver this message. He had never seen me or spoken to me before.

That afternoon, the pastor and four elders from my church came to visit me. Before they left, the pastor said, "Dan, we would like to pray for you, that God would heal you. Is that all right?"

"Is that all right?" I exclaimed. "That's what Diane and David and I have been trusting God to do! Please pray for me!"

As I lay on the living room sofa, the pastor knelt, as did two of the men. They all laid hands on me. Then the pastor prayed, "Our Father in heaven, we bring our brother before You. He needs Your healing touch. In the Name of Jesus Christ, through the power of Your Holy

Spirit, heal Dan from the crown of his head to the bottoms of his feet. We thank You and praise Your name. In Jesus' name we pray. Amen."

I moved in an effort to stand.

"No, Dan, don't get up," the pastor said. "We know how sick you are."

My voice was loud as I answered, "I have to see if God has *healed* me." I jumped off the couch and knew immediately, by my being able to do that, that something had indeed happened. I shouted, "The pain is gone!" and as I walked my friends to the door, I told them again that God had taken away my pain, that He had healed me.

I needed to take no more medication for pain from that moment on because I *had* no more pain, and in fact, the day after my healing, I was hiking across the fields of our three-hundred-acre estate, praising God for the energy and strength he had given me.

The Lord, in His mercy, had provided a sign. As a physician, a man of science, I knew that pain from tumor load in most of a person's skeleton did not naturally go away in an instant without any form of medical treatment. Even with a very good response to treatment of prostate cancer, it usually takes several months until bone pain decreases enough that narcotic pain medication can be stopped. The phenomenon that had occurred in my body I could explain only by the marvelous, supernatural power of God. Praise the Lord!

✣ ✣ ✣

CHAPTER 5

THE CRUSADE

> *And Elisha sent a messenger to him, saying,*
> *"Go and wash in the Jordan seven times,*
> *and your flesh shall be restored to you, and you shall be clean."*
> —*II Kings 5: 10*

In the next few days, our answering machine continued to record up to forty phone calls a day. It was a humbling thought to know how many Christians—it appeared to be thousands—were praying for me to be healed. If you who are reading this testimony were among those who prayed, I thank you.

One phone call was from a local Christian doctor who stated that he had just returned from a healing crusade and that God was delivering a lot of people from their illnesses there. Diane was listening with me to the answering machine message. "He thinks you should go to a crusade, Dan," she said.

"God has already healed me," I countered. "Do I need to be healed again?"

Over the next few weeks, many Christian friends came to visit me, and soon I began to hear, "We don't always know God's will" and "God doesn't heal everyone." It was discouraging to me to

Reach Out—Touch Him

hear these things from my Christian friends. The only solace for me was to bury myself in the Word of God. I read the Bible as much as seven or eight hours a day, underlining verses and reading them in prayer.

"Diane, look at this promise!" It was one of the many times a day that I would run into the kitchen to show her a Bible verse. I read:

> But He was wounded for our transgressions,
> He was bruised for our iniquities;
> The chastisement for our peace was upon Him,
> And by His stripes we are healed.

"That's Isaiah 53:5," I told her. "And look what it says about the healings in Matthew, Chapter Eight." I ran my finger from the second part of verse 16 through 17:

> And He cast out the spirits with a word, and healed
> all who were sick, that it might be
> fulfilled which was spoken by Isaiah the prophet, saying:
> "He Himself took our infirmities
> And bore our sicknesses."

"See? It's a physical healing, and it's part of the atonement Jesus made when he became our sacrifice," I explained in earnest.

One morning I was reading in Matthew, Chapter Seventeen, how a man came to Jesus asking for mercy on his epileptic son. Verse 16 read, "'So I brought him to your disciples, but they could not cure him.'" Jesus healed the boy.

I read through verses 19 and 20:

> Then the disciples came to Jesus privately and
> said, "Why could we not cast it out?"

The Crusade

> So Jesus said to them, "Because of your unbelief; for assuredly, I say to you, if you have faith as a mustard seed, you will say to this mountain, 'Move from here to there,' and it will move; and nothing will be impossible for you."

Faith as big as a mustard seed! That's all the faith I needed to have in order to "move" this "mountain." *That's how much I do have*, I thought as I headed for Diane, to share my discovery.

Passing by the fireplace, I had this certain knowledge within me, placed there by God Himself, I was sure: *There is no possibility that I'm not healed.* Standing in the kitchen holding each other close, Diane and I cried as I shared these thoughts with her.

A few minutes later the phone rang. It was the Christian doctor who had left a phone message two days before, telling me of a healing crusade. He greeted me and then asked whether I'd gotten that message.

"Yes," I replied, "but it was one of hundreds of phone calls."

"Do you know about healing crusades?" he asked.

"No."

"A friend and I went to a crusade in Toronto. As doctors, we thought it might be fake—but it wasn't!" He was talking with energy now. "We saw hundreds of people being healed. It was undeniable," he went on, his words coming in quick succession. "You could feel the power of the Holy Spirit. Dan, you have to go," he almost shouted. "God will heal you, and it will be a great testimony to the medical community!"

"Steve," I answered, "God has already healed me. My pastor and four elders from the church prayed for me in my home, and my pain left in an instant. I'm no longer on pain medicine."

"Go *anyway*," he pleaded. "You'll feel the power of the Holy Spirit, and it'll strengthen your faith to see others healed."

Reach Out—Touch Him

"How do I go?" I asked. My friend described the crusade he had attended. It was a television ministry, all new to me. We don't have a television set in our home because of the negative influence that it would have on our son, David, and we didn't know about television ministries such as this.

After I discussed my phone conversation with Diane, she suggested that I call my pastor brother, Dave. I dialed him and explained what my friend Steve had suggested. "Should I go?" I asked.

"The Lord has already healed you," Dave replied without hesitation.

"I know," I said. "Steve says it will encourage my faith."

"Then pray about it," Dave told me, "and go, if God leads you to go."

A few minutes later, my sister Nancy called. She is a television producer and had worked for seven years producing The 700 Club. I told her how Dave suggested I pray about going to this healing crusade I had heard about.

"I know someone at CBN[1] who may be able to help," Nancy said.

Twenty minutes later, Nancy called me back and told me that her friend Jackie, at CBN, would take me to the crusade in Puerto Rico in two weeks. Hotel and airline reservations and a front seat at the crusade next to Jackie were all arranged.

Less than an hour had passed since my doctor friend's phone call. I looked at Diane. "I feel like Naaman going to the Jordan River,"[2] I said. "Here I am, a man of science, trained in the field of surgery, and I'm not ashamed to demonstrate my belief in God's Word by going to a faith healing service."

Diane, looking at me through tear-filled eyes, nodded her head.

✣ ✣ ✣

CHAPTER 6

STRUGGLES WITH BELIEF AND DOUBT

"Little girl I say to you, arise."
Immediately the girl arose and walked around....
But He commanded them strictly that no one should know it,
and said that something should be given her to eat.
—Mark 5:41b, 42a, 43

I was getting stronger each day, and now I began to wonder what I should do about doctors and medications. It seemed to me that perhaps I should not go back to the doctor and not take any medicine. As Diane and I talked and prayed about this, I remembered my prayer to the Lord during medical school: "I'll do my best if You'll do the rest."

My doctor brother, Vic, arranged for me to be seen by a renowned specialist at Memorial Sloan-Kettering Cancer Institute in New York City. As we were leaving home on our way to this appointment, I said to Diane, "Maybe I don't even have to see this doctor." She heard puzzlement in my voice.

"What did you do in medical school?" she asked. "Didn't you have to do everything you could do, and only then would God do the rest?"

The Lord teaches us in His Word to be good stewards, we decided.[1] It seemed reasonable to me, then, that if God gave us

Reach Out—Touch Him

knowledge and medical skills, we should use them. Furthermore, we should stop doing anything that might worsen any less-than-fit condition. If an obese person, for example, asked God to deliver him or her from obesity, would God honor the prayer if the person continued to eat as much as he or she had eaten before? No, I reasoned; in this situation, that would be unfaithful stewardship.

The situation of the girl whom Jesus raised from the dead was different. She needed, following her deliverance from death, to be nourished and strengthened by the ingestion of food. Jesus did the reasonable thing: He commanded that she be given something to eat.[2]

Diane and I decided in all diligence to thank God for my healing and do all that we, ourselves, could think of to help me get well. We became alert to every step that seemed positive.

Soon Diane, David and I sat facing the doctor at Sloan-Kettering. "I'm afraid things do not look good for you, doctor," he said. "The treatments we use for prostate cancer have very little chance of doing any good in a person as young as you are with widespread, metastatic disease. The tissue slides from the biopsies done on you show a Gleason score-eight aggressive tumor," he continued somberly. "We can give you Cisplatin for six months, but it probably won't do any good. The medicine will make you sick and cause all your hair to fall out." He paused, then added, "Maybe you just want to go home, get as comfortable as possible with narcotics, and spend the seven months or so that you have to live with Diane and David."

"Doctor," I said, "my pain is gone, and I have not taken pain medicine since the men from my church prayed for me. Have you ever seen anyone whose pain went away like that?"

"No," he replied. "The pain only gets worse and worse."

"God took the pain away," I explained eagerly. "I've known Jesus Christ as my Lord and Savior since I was a little boy, and that's why we prayed to God for healing. …If I were to put forth the best effort I could, what should I do?"

Struggles with Belief and Doubt

"Take the treatment," the doctor replied. "Do you want to do that?"

Diane and I looked at each other and nodded together, giving our assent.

On the drive home, I said to Diane, "I know God healed me. Am I doubting Him by taking treatment?"

"You're not doubting God's miracle," she said. "Remember how Naaman had to go and wash in the Jordan River as the man of God commanded?[3] …And the blind man Jesus anointed by putting clay on his eyes? Jesus told him, 'Go, wash in the pool of Siloam.'[4] These men had to do their part," she said earnestly, "and I believe God wants us to do everything we know to do."

"Well, if it's a choice between trusting God or trusting the medication," I said with certainty, "I trust God. None of the doctors even believe that the treatment will do any good."

Seventeen days after my diagnosis was made, while we were at home getting ready to go to the healing crusade, the phone rang and the nurse from my local primary-care physician's office greeted Diane excitedly, "Mrs. Gordeuk?"

"Yes," Diane replied.

"We have your husband's PSA test result, and it is really great." Her voice was filled with wonder. "The PSA is 61!" she announced, then added quickly, "Now, don't get your hopes up too high. The doctor wants to repeat the test to be sure it's not a lab error."

To see a PSA level decrease from 1,300 to 61 in a little over two weeks was, for lack of a more emphatic word, astonishing.

I went back to the lab to repeat the test as the doctor ordered. The result was even lower: 27. Within the next two months, the PSA turned normal, and it is normal at the writing of this book, almost three years later.

Reach Out—Touch Him

Several days after I received the test result of 27, while we were eating breakfast, the doorbell rang and someone shouted, "Anybody there?" It was my general surgery partner, Dale. "How are you, Dan?" he asked.

"I'm fine, Dale. God has healed me—He really has! My pain is gone. I'm not taking any pain medicine, and my PSA has gone down to 27." I knew my partner was not a believer. "What do you think, doc?" I asked.

"Well, it looks like you dodged this bullet, Dan," he said.

I continued to testify to every colleague of mine with whom I spoke and to any physician who examined me. The wonderful news of God's healing power was a strange concept to the medical community in my hometown, but could it be true? The physicians would wait and see.

On the day before we were to fly to Puerto Rico, I was given a Cisplatin injection, and we spoke again with the doctor in New York.

"You'll feel like a truck ran over you, and your hair will all fall out," he warned once more.

"God has healed me, doctor," I replied. "Maybe God will protect me from the effects of the medicine." The doctor did not offer any encouragement about my future or the course of treatment that day.

As we arrived in Puerto Rico, I felt so tired I wanted only to lie in bed. Diane and David splashed in the water next to the hotel while I rested, and for nearly thirty hours I hardly got up. I noticed my hair all over the pillows, and when I took a shower, the drain of the tub was stopped by a handful of hair.

When Diane phoned Jackie in her room, she discovered that the vans for the evening service were full. Jackie suggested we wait until the next day to go to the crusade. I had two reasons, now, to stay in bed and rest—medicinal side effects and no space in the vans—but I looked at Diane and said, "We came to go to the crusade. Let's go."

Struggles with Belief and Doubt

As I drove toward the outdoor arena, Diane routed our way on the map. When we arrived, we were seated on chairs on a grassy field, perhaps seventy yards from the stage. I noticed that *everyone* was praising God. The pastor, an American wearing a Caribbean-style white suit, was leading the assembly in worship. He was looking up and saying, "For all that You do, we will be careful to give You all the praise, dear Jesus."

Diane and I, surrounded by Puerto Rican Christians, cried and cried and praised the Lord as we felt His presence.[5]

The next evening, sitting beside Jackie in the front row, I found it hard to keep my hands up to praise the Lord. Then, in a moment, the Holy Spirit came upon me. I was filled with new strength—the Holy Spirit was within me.[6] He gave me certain assurance that my healing was genuine and complete.

Staff members nearby came running to me. "What happened?" several asked together. "Something has happened to you," they said.

Don, the physician helping to choose testimonies of healing, said, "We've got to get you up on stage. People need to see this!"

I had not yet spoken to anyone. Now, as I stood facing the pastor on stage, I declared, "God has filled me with His Holy Spirit and witnessed to the certainty of my healing."

❖ ❖ ❖

CHAPTER 7

UNDERSTANDING GOD'S LOVE AND PROVISION FOR HEALING

*"Call upon Me in the day of trouble;
I will deliver you, and you shall glorify Me."*
—Psalm 50:15

The next morning, I realized the new strength that I experienced at the crusade had not left me. The Holy Spirit was filling my whole being with His presence. I remembered Psalm 50:15, the verse my brother Dave had given me: "Call upon Me in the day of trouble; I will deliver you, and you shall glorify Me." The glory of God had fallen upon me.

"Diane," I shouted from the shower, "my hair's not falling out. The drain's not getting stopped up with it anymore."

"That's great!" Diane called from the other room. "Maybe the Lord is giving you another sign by keeping that from happening."

As we toured Puerto Rico with its surrounding islands, I felt no more fatigue. I carried our bags on and off ferries and hiked for miles on the beaches. Now, we all played *together* in the warm ocean waters. And, whereas my doctor had predicted that I would lose all my hair, that never did happen; it altogether quit falling out. God, in His mercy and love, *had* given me new evidence of His mighty power: He had healed me of the side effects of the medication.

When I think back to when I first got sick, I remember feeling like a burden to my family. I wondered why God would even care about me—I was no longer any help to anyone. These thoughts troubled me. But the Lord showed me His great love through David.

If we were crossing the street, I would hold David's small hand in my much larger, stronger hand. David would pull to get away. "I can go myself, Daddy," he would say. But I would not let go; I would hold on firmly until we had crossed the street. There was not anything, in fact, that I would not do to keep my son safe. If he had happened into the path of a moving truck, I would have jumped out and pushed him to safety even if I were to be struck, myself. I wouldn't have hesitated for a second.

When I read Jesus' words in Matthew on the father-son relationship, they resonated in me with regard to my love for David:

> "[W]hat man is there among you who, if your son asks for bread, will give him a stone? Or if he asks for a fish, will he give him a serpent? If you then, being evil, know how to give good gifts to your children, how much more will your Father who is in heaven give good things to those who ask Him!"[1]

I now realized God's love for me as His son was greater than my love for my own son. How could there be any love so great as His?[2] I began to find rest and peace in His love.

When a person has a terminal illness, there is a psychological phenomenon that can occur, called denial. This means that even though you are going to die, you don't believe it. It is a trick of the mind. I could see that many of my friends, even my Christian friends, thought I was in denial. One day while reading God's Word and praying in the southwest bedroom of our house, I prayed, "Lord, am I in denial?"

My mind recalled that God declares in the book of Malachi, "I am the Lord; I do not change,"[3] and the psalmist writes, "He remembers His covenant forever, the word which He commanded, for a thousand generations."[4] At that moment, God gave me the certain knowledge that His promises are true and are fixed forever in the heavens.[5] Jesus states, further, that "the things which are impossible with men are possible with God."[6]

I was sure now that, just as I would hold my son's small hand in mine, my own hand was held fast in the large, strong hand of my Father—my *heavenly* Father. And as I walked hand in hand with the King of kings and Lord of lords, it did not matter if those around me spoke of denial or did not believe in God's healing power. *He* had healed me *anyway*. I was not ashamed to have my hand in His and to proclaim His glory to everyone who would listen.[7]

Even if all the priests, rabbis and ministers, together with all the scholars and theologians in the world today, were to agree that God does not and cannot heal anyone, God's promises would still be, and *are*, true and valid for that person who becomes like a child[8] and believes His Word. We do not find out what God's Word means by looking around us at other people. I have heard people say, "I knew of a dear Christian person who had as much faith as anyone can have; she trusted God to heal her, but she still died. So, you see, God does not promise to heal everyone."

The fact is, we don't know and cannot judge[9] anyone else's relationship with God. We do know that God has chosen to make promises to those who believe, and that He honors our simple, child-like

Reach Out—Touch Him

faith. We know that "Jesus Christ is the same yesterday, today and forever."[10] If there were only one person on earth who chose to believe God's promise, He would still keep His promise.

There is an example in God's Word of what happens when people refuse to believe that Jesus is the Son of God. When Jesus went to his hometown of Nazareth, people said:

> "Is this not the carpenter, the Son of Mary, and brother of James, Joses, Judas, and Simon? And are not His sisters here with us?" So they were offended at Him.
>
> But Jesus said to them, "A prophet is not without honor except in his own country, among his own relatives and in his own house." Now He could do no mighty work there, except that he laid His hands on a few sick people and healed them.[11]

Our world today is like Jesus' home country. We "know better" than to think that God actually heals people in the name of Jesus through the power of the Holy Spirit. We believe in science. We trust radioactive carbon dating. We know about the electron microscopic structure of cells. We've seen men walk on the moon and computers take the place of people's hands.

One woman actually said to me, when I asked her if she believed God could heal her, "I believe doctors can heal." By implication, she was saying that God could not heal disease. But when Jesus walked on earth, almost no one doubted His power to heal. The high priest, the scribes and the Pharisees all knew that Jesus could heal. It was Jesus' ability to forgive sins that they doubted.[12]

Today it seems popular to believe that Jesus can forgive our sins, but few believe that He can heal our sicknesses. One Christian physician asked me after hearing my testimony of healing, "What do you think happened to those cancer cells? Did the cell walls break up, or did the DNA fall apart?"

I considered his questions. As physicians, we use many drugs for which the mechanism of action is unknown. We know how to use the drugs and that the drugs work, but we don't know *how* they work. For these drugs, the PDR[13] states, "mechanism of action: unknown."

If we try to explain the mechanism of action of the power of God, we will fail. God's ways are above our understanding.[14] We will never be able to explain the mechanism of action of the power of the Holy Spirit. It is awesome, it is wonderful, and it works.

God delivers us from the spirit of the infirmity, as He delivered the woman who was bound by the power of Satan for eighteen years.[15] When the spirit of the infirmity is removed by God, the sickness goes away.[16] Praise Him for His mighty power and His faithfulness that "endures to all generations."[17]

❊ ❊ ❊

CHAPTER 8

CONFOUNDING THE DOCTORS: WELLNESS AND STRENGTH RETURN

*But those who wait on the L*ORD
Shall renew their strength;
They shall mount up with wings like eagles,
They shall run and not be weary,
They shall walk and not faint.
—Isaiah 40:31

Big Bend National Park, in South Texas, has a mountainous desert terrain with hiking trails and interesting sights.

"How much farther to the top?" I asked as we climbed a mountain trail.

"About a mile, I think," Diane answered, looking at her trail map.

Our son, David, walked with us, his eyes full of expectation, his hands full of rocks.

"Will we see a mountain lion, Daddy?" he asked. He had begun to collect rocks after we read a sign warning of possible mountain lions on the trail. "If we see a lion, I'll throw rocks at it. Then I'll jump up and down and shout and wave my arms," he announced.

Reach Out—Touch Him

Our family had gone south so that we would have little to interfere with exercising each day. Our thinking was that, following God's healing of my body, a daily seven-mile walk would help strengthen me faster.

The sun rose above our heads and the temperature climbed to 85°F. We decided to hike on another trail to the bottom of a mountain canyon. David soon fell asleep on my back as I carried him. The hiking was great, and at the end of the day Diane glanced at the park map and added up our hiking mileage.

"We walked eleven-and-a-half miles; we climbed 2,800 feet, and you carried David on your back about eight miles after he fell asleep," she said, eyes shining. "God has really restored your strength." This happened just over two months after God healed me.

A few days earlier, we had seen a doctor at Sloan-Kettering who was a nutrition specialist. While doing the routine history and physical examination that physicians are trained to do, he asked me, "Doctor, what do you take for pain?"

"Nothing," I said. "Two days after I was diagnosed, five men from my church came and prayed for me at my home. My pain went away as they prayed, and I haven't taken medicine for pain since."

A few minutes later, the doctor asked again, "What *pills*, doctor, do you take for pain?" He was holding his index finger and thumb in such a way as to describe the size of a pill.

"As I told you," I said, "I'm not taking pain pills. My pain left me as the five men from my church prayed for me."

A little later, the doctor turned to Diane. "What medication, ma'am, pain medication, does your husband take?"

"He is on no pain medication," Diane answered quietly.

One last time before ending his interview, the doctor asked me, "What pain medication do you take?"

"None since the men from my church prayed..." I started to answer.

Confounding the Doctors: Wellness and Strength Return

"I know," said the doctor with a whimsical look, "the pain left when the men prayed for you."

While the doctors were having trouble understanding why I had no pain, I was climbing mountains and hiking on trails with David on my back. Praise the Lord for his mighty miracle of supernatural healing!

One day, I heard the phone ring, and a moment later Diane called to me from the kitchen that there was a woman from the National Cancer Society who wanted to talk to me.

"Okay," I said, reaching for my desk phone.

"Could you speak at our March for Life at the high school football field?" the caller asked.

"Yes, I can," I answered.

After I hung up the phone, I sat thinking about how I had come so quickly and surely to that answer. I knew that God had healed me. As a physician, I reasoned that even though the PSA had turned normal, bone scans and CT scans would have to be done after a period of time to objectively demonstrate absence of cancer. I turned to Diane.

"I have to testify that God *has* healed me. When I go to the March for Life, I'll give my testimony and praise God for healing me!"

On the appointed evening, before several thousand people in the bleachers, I spoke of God's healing power and his miracle of restoring my body to health in the name of Jesus. After I finished my speech with the declaration, "Praise the Lord," people surrounded me, thanking me for the message of hope.

Soon we had requests to speak in dozens of churches in our community and even in other cities and states. It seemed to me that it was pleasing to the Lord for me to bear witness to His mighty miracle of healing me. The words in Psalm 50 kept coming to my mind: "Call upon Me in the day of trouble; I will deliver you, and you shall glorify Me."

I am not a fluent speaker. Soon, I was amazed to see that when I glorified God and lifted up Jesus, I was fluent, if not eloquent. This was a talent I had never possessed, and I knew that it was another miracle of God.

The book of Exodus pictures Moses uncertain before the Lord because he was "slow of speech and slow of tongue." But the Lord said, "Now therefore, go, and I will be with your mouth and teach you what you shall say."[1] The Holy Spirit was teaching my mouth what to say.

I felt quite humbled to think that God had healed me, trusting me to glorify Him afterward. What a blessing it was to praise Him and to demonstrate my faith in His healing power by publicly sharing my return to health through Jesus!

Diane and I also noticed that it was a great encouragement to our faith to be in places where many people were praising God and expecting to see miracles through the name of Jesus. I decided to write a letter in which I would offer to work as a physician at healing crusades just like the one where I had been healed of the side effects of my chemotherapy. We soon found ourselves traveling to many cities in this capacity.

One day, in a hotel lobby, I said to Joan, one of the crusade staff, "It's so exciting to be able to share what God has done for me. People from various churches are writing to ask me to come and give my testimony."

"You have no idea how the Holy Spirit will work through you," she said. "I can't even explain it now. You'll see."

Later I would find out what she meant. God would do "exceedingly and abundantly above" that which I would "ask or think."[2]

CHAPTER 9

GOD'S CALL

*Now, Lord…grant to Your servants that with
all boldness they may speak Your word,
by stretching out Your hand to heal, and that
signs and wonders may be done through
the name of Your holy Servant Jesus.* —Acts 4:29

"I have the bone scan results here," the doctor said, scarcely containing his excitement.

Diane, David and I were sitting before the same doctor at Sloan-Kettering who had told us six months earlier that I had seven months to live.

"Look at this, Dan," he continued. "The tumor is gone. The only abnormality you can see now is what you would expect to see from healing bone. …I expect you will do very well from here on out."

Indeed, there was no more talk of dying in the next month! The physical examination and CT scan both indicated that the prostate was now normal, even small, in size.

"I believe God has healed me in the name of Jesus Christ of Nazareth," I told my primary care physician as we reviewed these findings.

Reach Out—Touch Him

I continued to study God's Word diligently every day, sometimes for periods of many hours. It seemed as if I could not find out enough about God and His promises to us. Every time I read about God's deliverance, mercy and love toward His people, it helped me to know more about what He was like.

The faith of Abraham seemed to me a monumental, shining standard. Abram (as he was called before his encounter with God) did not have the Scriptures to read, nor did he know what God had done for other men. Yet when the Lord spoke to him and said, "Get out of your country…to a land that I will show you,"[1] the Bible tells us, "Abram departed as the Lord had spoken to him."[2]

Later, when Abram, now named Abraham, was old, the Lord said to him, "Sarah your wife shall have a son."[3] Sarah, well past the age of childbearing, laughed to herself. And the Lord said to Abraham, "Why did Sarah laugh, saying, 'Shall I surely bear a child, since I am old?' Is anything too hard for the Lord?"[4]

Abraham, however, believed the Lord, Who had said, "Look now toward heaven, and count the stars… So shall your descendants be."[5] Abraham's ultimate faith in God was demonstrated when God later tested him by saying, "Take now your son, your only son Isaac, whom you love, and go to the land of Moriah, and offer him there as a burnt offering on one of the mountains of which I shall tell you."[6] The following verse reads: "So Abraham rose early in the morning and saddled his donkey…."[7] He proceeded as God had directed. What faith this was! To someone who trusted God less, it would have seemed that He was not keeping His promise as Abraham obediently went to sacrifice Isaac early that morning. But God had made that promise, and He kept it. Isaac was spared, and Abraham's faith was vindicated.

Diane and I were having one of our customary talks in the kitchen one morning. "Look at Abraham," I said. "He had great faith, and God honored that when the situation seemed impossible. We can trust God like that."

"Everyone is not Abraham, Dan," Diane countered with a twinkle in her eye, and then we agreed: God is no respecter of persons,[8] and as our faith is, so it will be for us.[9]

Was it wrong to ask God for faith like Abraham's? I read in Luke 22: "And the Lord said, 'Simon, Simon! Indeed, Satan has asked for you, that he may sift you as wheat. But I have prayed for you that your faith should not fail.'"[10] Jesus was speaking to Peter prior to his own arrest and trial. He knew Peter would deny him, but He prayed for Peter's faith.

I continued to pray, "Jesus, strengthen my faith." It was scriptural, I saw, to ask God for more faith.

If you go to the doctor after God has healed you, you can be relatively sure that when you step up to the examining table and the doctor comes into the room, he won't say, "Praise the Lord—I see that God has healed you." A physician who does not know Jesus in a personal way does not have spiritual discernment. God's Word declares that spiritual things are spiritually discerned.[11] In working with a terminally ill patient, a doctor without spiritual discernment does not look at a test result and try to see how it is compatible with God's miracle of healing. Rather, he will repeat what he knows about the course of an incurable disease, complete with dismal statistics, and try to explain how a given test result fits this picture.

So, even though my health and the medical tests rapidly and continuously progressed toward normal after God healed me, the physicians I was seeing were slow to shift their emphasis away from what one would expect to happen to me if God had *not* healed me. It seemed important that I dwell on God's Word and His promises so that my faith, like Peter's, should not fail.

One day, as I studied the Scriptures and prayed, God spoke to me[12] with the thought, "It is enough, this continual strengthening of your faith; now, go, speak the word, and let Me work through you."

Reach Out—Touch Him

I read in my Bible, "Now, Lord...grant to Your servants that with all boldness they may speak Your word, by stretching out Your hand to heal, and that signs and wonders may be done through the name of Your holy Servant, Jesus."[13]

I am a physician, a general surgeon, not a minister. It was one thing to stand up and tell people about how I, like millions before me, had touched the hem of Jesus' garment, so to speak.[14] It was another matter for me to stand and speak His words through the power of the Holy Spirit in order that sick people be healed.

What if I were to do this and nothing happened?

I knew that God had healed me and purified my body as a temple of the Holy Spirit. I knew that I was filled with the Holy Spirit. I asked the Holy Spirit *every* morning to go with me through the day. Now, I decided, I would be obedient to Him. I would stand forth and speak the word in faith so that people could be healed. It was up to God what He would do.

Tanned and apparently healthy, Dan celebrates his first Fathers Day, in June, 1994, with baby David.

Christmas, 1996. A kiss from two-year-old David for Daddy, who is not at all well.

Reach Out—Touch Him

Trusting in God's intervention and His promises from Scripture, the Gordeuks head to Clearwater Beach, Florida in March of 1997. Here Dan can walk every day in good weather to recoup his strength in muscles that have atrophied.

At first, Dan spends more time on the bed in the family camper than on the beach. But by the end of his stay, he is ready to hike; vitality and strength have resurged.

September, 2001. Dan offers his old tractor for display at the Antique Machinery Show in Centre Hall, Pa. and enjoys the event with David and Diane.

David's home-schooling portrait, October, 2001. Photo by Wal-Mart.

Reach Out—Touch Him

Enjoying a full life, with Diane, 2001.

Reclaiming the fun of beach outings with Diane and David (covered in sand to his neck) on vacation in Hawaii, May, 2002. Diane again wields the camera.

Family fishing trip the next month (June, 2002) to Québec, Canada—an all-round success.

Dan (center) and David hiking in Alaska the same summer—August, 2002.

Reach Out—Touch Him

Interstate 99 allowed biking the day before it officially opened in October, 2002. Here, Dan and David break for a photo on the section that bypasses State College, Pa.

Tapping maple trees for syrup on the Gordeuk farm property, February, 2003. Dan had returned to the woods six years earlier to hunt, fully reclaiming his zest for life and feelings of restored well-being.

On safari with friends in 2004, Dan shows David vast new horizons in Zimbabwe. As is her custom, Diane is behind the camera.

✤ ✤ ✤

CHAPTER 10

THE HOLY SPIRIT SPEAKS TO ME

Also, I heard the voice of the Lord, saying:
"Whom shall I send,
And who will go for Us?"
Then I said, "Here am I! Send me."
—Isaiah 6:8

"That car is going into the ditch, Dad!" I exclaimed. I was a young boy riding beside my father in our station wagon. As we watched, the car ahead of us slipped left, then right. It came to rest in the drainage ditch beside the road. Snow was falling as we got out of our car to see if we could help.

"Are you all right?" my father asked, looking intently at the driver.

As the middle-aged man turned away from my father's gaze, I could see on his cheeks and forehead deep fresh scratches that were bleeding. The woman with him was coming toward us from the door on the passenger side. She looked so angry that I suspected their car had not slipped off the road because of the light snow cover, but rather that the man had lost control because he was fighting with his wife.

Reach Out—Touch Him

My dad seemed to have forgotten why we had stopped. "Sir, you need the Lord!" he said, holding the man by his coat lapels and shaking him. "You need to ask Jesus to forgive you of your sins."

I was astonished to notice that the man looked at my dad as though he expected this kind of treatment and deserved the admonition.

"What I mean is that you need to *pray* and ask Jesus to forgive you of your sins," my dad repeated.

The man nodded thankfully and said he would ask Jesus for forgiveness. Now my dad released his grip on the man's clothes, and we all worked to get the car out of the ditch.

As we drove toward home afterward, I asked, "Dad, why did you do that?"

"The Lord wanted me to talk to the man about his soul," Dad explained. "I just had to do it."

One month later, this rough and tumble man whom my father had confronted and urged to repent—a man in the strength of middle age—was killed in an auto accident. If he had followed through on his intentions and claimed Jesus as his Savior, then his salvation had come in the nick of time.

Several other times, my dad had spoken to me of God's direct leading in his life, and following each event I had seen notable consequences occur, evidently as a result. Sometimes God spoke to my dad. I knew it but did not understand it. God did not speak to me.

People sometimes ask, "What do you mean when you say, 'God spoke to him'?" In the field of psychiatry, this statement from a patient is often evidence of a delusional state. Does God actually speak to people on earth? The fact is He does, in several ways.

We know through biblical history that God spoke, directly or through His Angel, to Noah, Abraham, Isaac, Jacob, Moses, Elijah, and Samuel and, through his prophets and priests, to David and many others.

Later, when Jesus walked the earth, He assured his followers, "I will not leave you orphans."[1] He promised to send the Holy Spirit, the Spirit of truth.[2] "He," Jesus declared, "will teach you all things."

When we read God's Word, it is not like reading the newspaper. The Holy Spirit teaches us, shows us things. It is a miracle. This is the primary way that the Holy Spirit talks to us today.

Before his ascension, Jesus commanded His disciples "not to depart from Jerusalem but to wait for the Promise of the Father, which," He said, "you have heard from Me, for John truly baptized with water, but you shall be baptized with the Holy Spirit not many days from now."[3] He also promised power "when the Holy Spirit has come upon you."[4] While the apostles waited in one accord in obedience to Jesus' command, they heard "a sound...as of a mighty, rushing wind," were "filled with the Holy Spirit" and "began to speak with other tongues, as the Spirit gave them utterance."[5] These were both spiritual and physical phenomena.

We remember that physical and spiritual phenomena also accompanied God's speaking to and through the Old Testament patriarchs. His instructions to Noah prior to the Great Flood, His warnings to Abraham concerning the impending destruction of Sodom and Gomorrah, His call to Moses through the burning bush, and His deliverance of the Children of Israel through the ten plagues He pronounced upon Egypt through Moses are just a few examples.

Is it too much then, to expect God to communicate to us today through both physical and spiritual means? Has God changed? God's Word declares in Malachi 3:6: "...I am the LORD, I do not change...."

After God healed me and purified my body, it became a temple of the Holy Spirit.[6] God healed me so that I could glorify Him,[7] and later, I sensed the Holy Spirit filling my body. God does not heal us so that we can live a hedonistic life full of sinful pleasures.[8] He heals us so that we can serve and glorify Him. He fills us with His Holy Spirit so that He can guide us into fruitful service and abundant, joyous living.

What happens when a person is filled with the Holy Spirit? Is it a subtle, unnoticeable event? What Jesus did in Matt. 10:1 was not subtle: "And when He had called his twelve disciples to Him, He gave them power over unclean spirits, to cast them out, and to heal all kinds of sickness and diseases." The Bible records the words of Jesus in Mark 16:17: "And these signs will follow those who believe: In my name they will cast out demons. They will speak with new tongues; they will take up serpents and if they drink anything deadly, it will by no means hurt them; they will lay hands on the sick and they will recover."

The Holy Spirit guides us in a personal way so that His power can work through us. God's Word gives us an example in Acts, Chapter Eight.[9] An angel of the Lord told the deacon Philip to go south along the road from Jerusalem to Gaza. Philip walked south as directed, and when he came within sight of a certain chariot, the Spirit said to him, "Go near and overtake this chariot." So Philip started running. The Spirit had already prepared a high official of Ethiopia to interact with Jesus' follower: as he traveled, the Ethiopian eunuch was reading Isaiah, Chapter 53. Philip now saw why he was to walk this road and then run to this man; he asked him if he understood what he was reading, and the man promptly invited him to join him in the chariot. Philip preached Jesus to the Ethiopian, who accepted the message and was baptized. Then the Spirit caught Philip away and put him down on a street in Azotus.

So, God spoke to Philip through His Holy Spirit, and because God is no respecter of persons,[10] His gifts and promises apply to *all* those who believe Him and accept what He has offered. If we invite the Holy Spirit into our lives each day, and if we obey Him every time He shows us what to do, He will be our constant companion and best friend.

Young Samuel heard a voice as a little boy, while sleeping in his room in the temple. The Lord spoke to Samuel three times before Eli the priest recognized Who was speaking to his young helper.[11] Chapter Two of I Samuel explains that Eli and his family had sinned. Perhaps that is why "the word of the Lord was rare in those days" and "there was no widespread revelation."[12]

Samuel did not yet know the Lord so as to recognize His voice. After he came to know the voice of God, the Lord spoke to him many times throughout his long life as judge, priest, and prophet. God spoke directly to Samuel when He instructed him in the anointing of the first two kings of Israel.

In order to hear from God, we must be obedient to Him and seek Him daily. As the Holy Spirit speaks to us repeatedly, His messages become more and more familiar and are easier to discern. After I was healed and filled with the Holy Spirit, I sought to hear from Him each day. This was of vital importance if I was going to stand forth and speak the word in faith, allowing the Holy Spirit to work through me.[13] I continued to read God's Word each day and to invite the Holy Spirit to go with me and work through me.

I began to pray daily, "Let me be the man." I would tell the Lord, as Isaiah did after he was purged with the coal from the fire, "Here am I. Send me."[14]

The Holy Spirit began to give me insight into events around me so that, like Philip, who had spoken to the Ethiopian, I could speak about God's gift of eternal life to people He had prepared to receive my message.

Also, I noticed that often each day, while making a decision, I would have perfect inner peace about one course of action but unrest within me about the alternative.

Reach Out—Touch Him

The Holy Spirit was speaking to me in four ways:

1. Through God's Word
2. By providing insight into events around me
3. Through peace versus unrest about which course of action to choose
4. By bringing thoughts to my mind to facilitate my choice of direction.

And now, through the work of the Holy Spirit in my life, I have seen hundreds of miracles that are just as difficult to explain, in logical human terms, as was the miracle of my healing so long ago.

✣ ✣ ✣

CHAPTER 11

TESTAMENT

"...he who believes in Me, the works that I do he will do also; and greater works than these he will do...."
—*John 14:12a*

One year and three months after the Lord healed me, my family was vacationing in Arizona. As a guest in the local church, I heard the minister speak on Sunday morning. "My wife has cancer," he was saying. "God has given the doctors knowledge to put her on Tamoxifen,[1] and she has gotten better" were his glowing words. "We thank God for the extra time He has given her to be with us." Now, looking downcast, he continued, "But we know that this cancer will eventually come back and claim my dear wife's life, and then God in His mercy will take her to be with Him."

I could hardly wait to talk to the minister after the service. "Pastor," I said while shaking his hand, "I believe God wants to *heal* your wife." He looked at me, astounded. I told him of my incurable cancer, which God took away through the name of Jesus.

"I'll tell her," he said.

The next Sunday morning as I was leaving the service, a dignified woman in her sixties, tastefully arrayed in the finery befitting

Reach Out—Touch Him

the occasion, appeared by my side. She spoke almost timidly. "My husband told me you said God wants to heal me." With her was her friend, a slender woman of great optimism as it turned out.

"Yes," I said quietly. Then I told her of my impossible problem, which God had cured, and that with God all things are possible.[2] I mentioned the healing scriptures in Isaiah 53:5, Matthew 8:16, and Psalm 103:1-3.[3] Then I reminded her of Peter and John at the temple gate called Beautiful, where a man, lame from his mother's womb, asked alms of them. I repeated the text, "Then Peter said, 'Silver and gold I do not have, but what I do have I give you: In the name of Jesus Christ of Nazareth, rise up and walk.'"[4]

"That's it—it's for you!" exclaimed her friend.

Then I said, "An operation, radiation treatment and medication I do not have, but what I do have I give you: In the name of Jesus Christ of Nazareth, may your cancer leave and may you be healed from your head to your feet."

With this, the pastor's wife staggered and almost fell, but her friend caught her. A glowing smile of amazement spread over her face. "I was afraid to ask Him," she said. "I thought God was getting glory by my being sick."

I had begun to speak the word. When the Holy Spirit had impressed on me that I should do this and let Him work through me, I realized that saying yes to Him would put me at risk. I, a general surgeon, a man of science, was speaking the word so that in the name of Jesus, through the power of the Holy Spirit, people who believed might be healed.

Once again, doubt tried to move in. What would my colleagues think of me? What would *everyone* think? ...What if no one was healed?

Upon reflecting on all these questions, I realized that God had made the promises for healing, and it was He Who would demonstrate His ability to keep them and His faithfulness to do so. I was only a small instrument to be used by Him—a bystander privileged to catch glimpses of His mighty power. I was not going out on a limb by acting on the basis of God's promise to heal, because God was there in reality and power.

As I pondered the words of the pastor's wife—"I thought God was getting glory by my being sick"—I remembered what Jesus said in John 14:12-14:

> "Most assuredly, I say to you, he who believes in Me, the works that I do he will do also; and greater works than these he will do, because I go to My Father. And whatever you ask in My name, that I will do, *that the Father may be glorified* in the Son. If you ask anything in My name, I will do it." *(Emphasis mine)*

Jesus would do mighty things *to glorify God.* Although God can bring glory to His Name through the sick person's reliance on His strength, God receives the greater glory by healing His children. This principle is seen in the description of Abraham in Romans 4:20, 21.

> He did not waver at the promise of God through unbelief, but was strengthened in faith, giving glory to God, and being fully convinced that what He had promised He was also able to perform.

Thank the Lord for his faithfulness to keep His promises. Thank the Lord that He has chosen to bring glory to Himself by "signs and wonders" done through the name of Jesus.[5]

God had begun to use me, and He would continue to use me if I would be obedient to the Holy Spirit every time He showed me what to do. More than that, morning by morning as I invited the Holy

Reach Out—Touch Him

Spirit to come with me and work through me that day—although I didn't realize it then—God was readying me for a journey of faith I was to take that would remind me of Abraham's journey with his young son, Isaac.

✤ ✤ ✤

CHAPTER 12

OVERCOMING

> *He did not waver at the promise of God through unbelief, but was strengthened in faith, giving glory to God, and being fully convinced that what He had promised, He was also able to perform.*
> —Romans 4:20, 21

"Your PSA level, doctor, is 0.7." The lab technician was speaking to me on the phone. Her voice was soft and matter of fact, but it went through me like an electric shock. My PSA had been 0.2 or less for more than a year-and-a-half since God had healed me; now it had risen. I called my brother Vic.

"I believe Dr. Gordeuk is on rounds," said the receptionist. "Let me page him."

It was a long, anxious wait until I heard Vic's voice on the line. I came straight at him. "My PSA has gone up to 0.7, Vic. What do you think?"

"I'll call the folks at Sloan-Kettering, M. D. Anderson, and Northwest Hospital," he said.

Vic got back to me later that day. "I talked to physicians in New York, Houston, and Seattle," he told me. "They think your cancer has come back. They want to repeat all the studies."

Reach Out—Touch Him

"Vic," I answered, "God has healed me."

"I know," he said, "but let the doctors check you. It'll be good to establish why the PSA is going up."

"I'll go see the doctors," I told him, "but my faith is in the Lord!"

As I spoke with Diane about the elevated lab test result, I had an analogy on my mind. I said, "I feel like Abraham going back to sacrifice Isaac. When God gave Isaac to Abraham and Sarah in their old age,[1] He was fulfilling His promise through a supernatural miracle. Then, when the child was older and He asked Abraham to sacrifice his son of promise,[2] it seemed that everything would be lost—that God's promise to Abraham, to number his descendants as the stars in the sky, would be void."

"God keeps His promises, Dan." Diane spoke with quiet authority.

"I know," I said with growing fervor. "God was keeping His promise to Abraham, but His plan couldn't be *seen* by human eyes. All the natural indications pointed to Abraham's seed being lost."

Diane looked at me expectantly.

"God provided a ram for Abraham's sacrifice," I continued, "just as Abraham was about to prove his ultimate obedience to God."[3] I was preaching to the choir—Diane was nodding with tear-filled eyes—and as I waded and swam through discovery, I realized I was talking to myself as much as to her. "God is going to use this PSA elevation for His glory and as a testimony to others that He keeps His promises of healing even if the lab tests *don't* seem to demonstrate it."

Within three weeks, the doctors repeated a bone scan and a CT scan of the abdomen and pelvis, and the doctors at M. D. Anderson in Houston, Texas did eight prostate biopsies. The bone scan was now normal—no sign of cancer. The CT scan showed no cancer. Eight biopsies of the prostate showed no cancer. The biopsies showed some growth of new prostate cells and some inflammation. This explained the slight elevation in my PSA.

Overcoming

The PSA repeated a month later was 0.3. As if this were not good news enough, doctors in Seattle, Washington decided to do six more prostate biopsies, and these all showed no cancer.

Praise the Lord. Diane and I felt as though we had been tested very much as Abraham had. God had been faithful to His promise, and now we could praise Him even more.

As I mentioned earlier in the book, when God healed me, I wondered if I should not do anything the doctors suggested. After all, I was healed! Now I could see that God was using the medical technology employed by doctors who doubted my healing to give *documentation* to it.

Diane hung up the phone. "I just talked to a nurse from our hospital who has cancer. She wants to know what you did to get rid of yours. She thinks you got some alternative form of treatment in Mexico." Her eyes moist, she continued, "Dan, even the medical people see the miracle. I think the more tests they do on you, the more they'll see that God must have done something for you."

Vic, my oncologist brother, had seen evidence of this. He had arranged for his high-powered colleagues around the country to see me, and from all of this, God had gotten more glory.

I am reminded once again of the word of our God in Malachi 3:6: "...I am the Lord, I do not change...."

✤ ✤ ✤

CHAPTER 13

HEALING THE SICK AND DYING

Then He said, "Do not draw near this place.
Take your sandals off your feet,
for the place where you stand is holy ground."
—*Exodus 3:5*

"Does that phone have to ring all day?" Diane mused out loud as she went into the kitchen to pick up the receiver. In a moment, she told me who was calling and handed it to me.

My friend Greg greeted me, then queried, "Can you come with me to pray for my brother?"

"Yes. When do we go?" It was early in the week, and I had promised to fly to Anaheim, California on Thursday to work as physician at a healing crusade.

"Can you come Saturday?" he asked.

The trip from central Pennsylvania to Greenville, North Carolina, where Greg's brother was dying, would take nine hours. "I can come, Greg, but I'll have to meet you in Charlotte," I answered. "I'll be in California Thursday and Friday. Can you pick me up at the airport in Charlotte on Saturday?"

It was all arranged. Following my two days in Anaheim, Greg met my flight at Charlotte. As we walked to his van, he told me his brother was not doing well at all, and so on the drive to Greenville we prayed for the Holy Spirit's guidance.

I'll never forget the feeling that came over me as we entered the living room where Greg's brother lay on a recliner. There was a single step down to the floor level, but it felt to me as if we had descended seven or eight steps and were surrounded by an impenetrable air of gloom. Family members in the room seemed to meld with it.

After explaining to Greg's brother, in detail, the plan of salvation through Jesus Christ, I began to pray, "Father in Heaven, in the name of Jesus, defeat the power of Satan...." I could scarcely believe what I was saying. It seemed to be directed by the Holy Spirit. "We bind the power of Satan in this house in the name of Jesus Christ," I continued.[1]

The dying man then prayed these words after me: "Dear Jesus, forgive me of my sins. I need you because you died for me. I repent, the best I know how. I accept you, Jesus, as ruler of my life. Thank you for eternal life. ...In Jesus' name I pray. Amen."

The power of God came into the room like a fresh, cleansing breeze. It no longer seemed dark and gloomy, and now, as the Holy Spirit melted hearts and healed relationships in this family,[2] we seemed to be on a floor elevated above its surroundings. I felt as if I were standing on holy ground.

Thinking that I was just a doctor with no right to be there, I left the room. What a glorious time of love, victory and reconciliation this was for their family. Greg's brother rejoiced because he knew that God had done the greatest miracle, that of changing him into a new person, with sins forgiven and with the promise of eternal life. He had just become alive spiritually, and it was evident to those around him.[3]

We began our nine-hour drive back to Pennsylvania at 8:00 o'clock that evening. For several hours, as we motored through the night, the one taking his turn in the passenger seat could not sleep

Healing the Sick and Dying

a wink because of what had happened at the home we had just left. It seemed as though the glow of the presence of the Holy Spirit was with us even in the van while we drove.

It was 5:30 AM when I arrived home, just in time to shower and get ready to visit a mainline church near Lewistown, Pennsylvania.

"Can you stay awake to drive?" Diane asked as she covered David with a blanket and buckled him into his car seat.

"Yes. I don't feel sleepy. I'm still in awe of what the Lord did last night."

As I got out of our Suburban on the gravel parking lot of the church at which I was to give my testimony, the stressful schedule and sleep deprivation of the past four days seemed to come on me all at once in a wave of fatigue. Diane was changing David from "jammies" into his clothes.

"If the Lord works through me to touch someone today," I said, "there is *no way* I can take credit for anything. I feel totally spent. There is no spark of energy or imagination left in me."

As we entered the church, we felt the presence of God. The minister had chosen hymns of healing. The scripture was Psalm 103:1-3:

> Bless the LORD, O my soul;
> And all that is within me, bless His holy name!
> Bless the LORD, O my soul,
> And forget not all His benefits:
> Who forgives all your iniquities,
> Who heals all your diseases....

The morning prayer that followed was one of expectation for healing.

As I shared my testimony, I realized that the energy and flow of ideas and scriptures were not my own but from the Holy Spirit. It seemed a privilege to be there and to see God work.

Reach Out—Touch Him

When I had concluded and led a prayer for salvation, I felt drawn to speak the word of healing.⁴ I prayed, "In the name of Jesus, through the power of the Holy Spirit, may those of you who are sick be made well. We give all the glory to God." Then I motioned to the pastor to replace me. In front of the first pew I stood with the congregation, face forward, head bowed and eyes closed. The pastor's benediction did not come. Instead, to my surprise, someone tapped me on the shoulder and pointed to the altar. It was lined with people!

"They want you to pray for them," whispered the pastor.

As we prayed, a young lady accepted Jesus as her Savior. A middle-aged woman told me of the arthritis in her knees and of her frozen right shoulder, which she had not been able to move for more than a year. A venerable white-haired gentleman asked God to heal his heart; he had angina with exercise.

What happened cannot be humanly explained. The power of the Holy Spirit came upon those seeking healing. The white-haired man with angina jumped up and shouted, "My heart—I felt it 'turn a flip.' It's healed!" This was done with all his friends, family and neighbors looking on. He was not afraid to declare to all who would listen that God had supernaturally healed him.

As I turned to look at a scene of activity in the middle aisle of the church, I saw there the woman who had come to the altar because of arthritis in her knees and a frozen right shoulder. She was almost dancing, more or less waltzing gracefully down the aisle, swinging her right arm as a baseball pitcher would, and praising God: "My arm—I can move it! Look what God has done."

For the second time in less than twenty-four hours, I felt as if I were standing on holy ground. Considering myself unworthy, just a doctor, I quietly slipped outside during what I thought would be the benediction time, if the pastor chose to pronounce it. I didn't want anyone to say thank you. All the thanks needed to go to God, Who deserves all glory and praise.

As we started off in our Suburban, the young man who had invited me to speak at his church came rushing over to our open window. "The man who was healed of heart disease is running up and down the stairs to show everyone that he has no more angina," he said, out of breath from his own run to catch up with us. We praised God together.

"Wow" was Diane's whisper as I pressed my foot to the gas pedal, moving our little family, in stunned wonder, toward home.

CHAPTER 14

STEPS TO BELIEF, HEALING AND MAINTENANCE

Is anyone among you sick? Let him call for the elders of the church, and let them pray over him, anointing him with oil in the name of the Lord. And the prayer of faith will save the sick, and the Lord will raise him up. And if he has committed sins, he will be forgiven.
—*James 5:14, 15*

Our phone was still ringing frequently, but now with new purpose.

"Dr. Gordeuk?" a man's voice asked. He sounded far away. "My name's Dan, and I'm calling from California. I have cancer, and I want to trust God to heal me. Can you pray for me?"

We arranged to meet a few days later in the Midwest. He and his preacher brother listened for an hour as I outlined the scriptures on healing that I had learned.

"Can you write these verses down for me?" Dan asked.

"Yes," I answered, already writing.

I share these same scriptures here, so that those who want to trust God for healing can learn of His plan for them. You have encountered many of these passages in the course of reading my testimony.

Reach Out—Touch Him

1. Isaiah 53:5: But He was wounded for our transgressions,
   He was bruised for our iniquities;
   The chastisement for our peace was upon Him,
   And by His stripes we are healed.

2. Matthew 8: 16, 17: When evening had come, they brought to Him many who were demon-possessed. And He cast out the spirits with a word, and healed all who were sick, that it might be fulfilled which was spoken by Isaiah the prophet, saying:

   > "He Himself took our infirmities
   > And bore our sicknesses."

3. Matthew 21:22: "And whatever things you ask in prayer, believing, you will receive."

4. Psalm 50:15: "Call upon Me in the day of trouble; I will deliver you, and you shall glorify Me."

5. Psalm 103:1-3: Bless the Lord, O my soul;
   and all that is within me, bless His holy name!
   Bless the Lord, O my soul,
   and forget not all His benefits:
   Who forgives all your iniquities,
   Who heals all your diseases….

6. John 14:12-14: "Most assuredly, I say to you, he who believes in Me, the works that I do he will do also; and greater works than these he will do, because I go to My Father. And whatever you ask in My name, that I will do, that the Father may be glorified in the Son. If you ask anything in My name, I will do it."

Steps to Belief, Healing and Maintenance

7. Malachi 3:6: "For I am the Lord; I do not change...."

8. Luke 18:27: But He said, "The things which are impossible with men are possible with God."

9. Mark 1:40-41: Now a leper came to Him, imploring Him, kneeling down to Him and saying to Him, "If You are willing, You can make me clean."

    Then Jesus, moved with compassion, stretched out His hand and touched him, and said to him, "I am willing; be cleansed."

10. Matthew 17:14-21: ...A man came to Him, kneeling down to Him and saying, "Lord, have mercy on my son, for he is an epileptic and suffers severely; for he often falls into the fire and often into the water. So I brought him to Your disciples, but they could not cure him."

    Then Jesus answered and said, "O faithless and perverse generation, how long shall I be with you? How long shall I bear with you? Bring him here to Me." And Jesus rebuked the demon, and it came out of him; and the child was cured from that very hour.

    Then the disciples came to Jesus privately and said, "Why could we not cast it out?"

    So Jesus said to them, "Because of your unbelief; for assuredly, I say to you, if you have faith as a mustard seed, you will say to this mountain, 'Move from here to there,' and it will move; and nothing will be impossible for you. However, this kind does not go out except by prayer and fasting."

Reach Out—Touch Him

11. Isaiah 45:118, 119: For thus says the Lord,
    "...I have not spoken in secret,
    In a dark place of the earth;
    I did not say to the seed of Jacob,
    'Seek Me in vain';
    I, the Lord, speak righteousness.
    I declare things that are right."

12. Matthew 7:9-11: "Or what man is there among you who, if his son asks for bread, will give him a stone? Or if he asks for a fish, will he give him a serpent? If you then, being evil, know how to give good gifts to your children, how much more will your Father who is in Heaven give good things to those who ask Him!"

13. Acts 14:8-10: And in Lystra a certain man without strength in his feet was sitting, a cripple from his mother's womb, who had never walked. This man heard Paul speaking. Paul, observing him intently and *seeing that he had faith to be healed*, said with a loud voice, "Stand up straight on your feet!" And he leaped and walked. (*Emphasis mine*)

14. James 5:14, 15 (Please see passage at the head of this chapter.)

When I was dying, without hope from medical forms of treatment, Diane and I wanted to trust God for healing. We did not know how to do it or what to do. The Holy Spirit has been faithful to me, revealing God's plan of healing through the scriptures.[1]

I would like to outline for you the steps you must take to trust God for your healing.

Steps to Belief, Healing and Maintenance

1. Seek to learn about the promises God made to His children for healing. Read these scriptures over and over until the Holy Spirit has made the truth of God's promises real to you.

2. Make sure you have confessed your sins and asked Jesus Christ to forgive you of them.[2]

3. If you have any unforgiveness or hatred—or an unloving spirit—toward anyone who has wronged you, ask their forgiveness.[3] Ask God to give you love for that person.

4. Call for the elders of the church to pray over you and anoint you with oil in Jesus' name, for healing and forgiveness, as prescribed in James 5:14, 15.[4]

5. Tell your family and friends that God has healed you.[5]

6. Read the Word of God and pray daily for as long as it takes for the Holy Spirit to speak to you.[6]

7. Pray each day in Jesus' name that your faith will remain sure.[7]

8. Try to surround yourself with Christians who believe in God's power to heal.[8]

9. Remember Malachi 3:6: God does not change.

10. Invite the Holy Spirit to fill your temple (body), which God has purified.[9]

11. Do not do anything that you know God does not want you to do, but live your life for the glory of God.[10, 11]

✣ ✣ ✣

CHAPTER 15

RETROSPECTION

*For the Scripture says,
"Whoever believes on Him will not be put to shame."
—Romans 10:11*

After I was healed, it was an active process for me to gain and maintain strong faith. The day after my healing, a minister came to my home and stressed to me that I should be studying God's Word to learn more about heaven because I would be going there soon. He was the first of a long list of Christian friends and ministers who would come to me and express their doubt about God's healing me.

Indeed, it *was* necessary for me to study the Word because, in fact, it was the most important *refuge from doubt* that I had. God's Word in Isaiah declares, "You will keep him in perfect peace, whose mind is stayed on You...."[1]

As I mentioned earlier, I studied the Scriptures each day, sometimes for seven or eight hours. It was as I studied that I learned of Jesus' prayer for Peter. "Satan has asked for you, that he may sift you as wheat," Jesus told his disciple. "But I have prayed for you, that your faith should not fail."[2] As I've stated, in this straightforward statement I saw that I could ask God in Jesus' name not to let my faith fail. I did this every day. If God was willing to keep Peter's faith strong, He would also do it for me, because He shows no partiality.[3]

As long as I was studying the promises God made to His children for healing, I was not doubting God's miracle of healing. I also began to learn more about the character of God and what He has revealed in His Word about His sovereign will. As discussed in the previous chapters of this book, God makes His will clear regarding the *salvation* of all who will accept His gift of eternal life. God's provision for *healing* His people is also clear. Following His scourging, Jesus died on the cross, offering up His perfect life, his very blood, to take away our sins, give us peace and provide for our healing.[4]

After God healed me, I was soon strong and well. Diane and I found that if we went to Florida, where we could regularly exercise in the warm weather, no one ever asked if I was sick. I did not look sick; I looked normal and strong. It was good for us to get away from the people who doubted my healing and to be around people, instead, who could tell by looking at me that I was well.

I used every opportunity I had to testify about God's wonderful healing of my body, and each time, I did it to the glory of God.[5] When I saw a doctor, I always told him that God had healed me. My testimonies to physicians and others began before six months had passed—the time at which follow-up bone scans and CT scans would be done. I felt that if I was faithful to glorify God[6], He would not let me down.[7] He would keep His promise.

Diane, David and I attended church services where people praised God and believed that He always kept His promises. We often attended healing crusades. When 20,000 people came together in one place to praise God and invite the Holy Spirit to work in Jesus' name, it was good for me to be there. I found it wonderful to witness the evidence of the power of the Holy Spirit, and seeing God heal other people strengthened my faith. Diane felt the same way.

Retrospection

Every time I had a doctor's appointment, the natural course of advanced prostate cancer would be on my mind. The doctors never said anything about God's power to heal. They only repeated what they had been taught in their training—training which did not include God's power to heal. As I listened to them, I would begin to think like a doctor. This was not the way to keep my eyes on Jesus. After every doctor's appointment, I would revisit God's promises.

The accounts of Abraham and Moses came to me many times. I would review how God had spoken to Abram before he named him Abraham. Abram trusted God and obeyed Him.[8] Abram did not have the Scriptures as we do, with all of God's promises and accounts of how He kept them if people believed and trusted Him. The Lord came to Abram in a vision, promising protection and great reward.[9]

All the doctors specializing in prostate cancer who examined me told me that I was in uncharted waters. They had never seen anyone like me get well before and, therefore, could not give me any advice based on previous experience. Until this time, I had very little knowledge, myself, of anyone's being healed. I could, however, look back on Abraham and see how he trusted God when no one around him had ever heard of trusting God—and how God kept His promise to Abraham, giving him a son and innumerable descendants because "he believed in the LORD, and He accounted it to him for righteousness."[10] I resolved to believe and trust God for my healing even if the prevailing belief of some Christians was that God might not heal me. This was no different from the way Abraham had stood alone on faith in God.

I learned another lesson from Moses. The Angel of the Lord appeared to Moses in a burning bush.[11] Then the Lord spoke to Moses, commanding "Take your sandals off your feet, for the place where you stand is holy ground."[12] God identified Himself to Moses as "I AM WHO I AM,"[13] and Moses was obedient to the Lord, trusting Him and acting on his faith. I resolved to do the same. God had gotten my undivided attention through prostate cancer, as He had Moses' through the burning bush. I would trust I AM WHO I AM, the Living God.

Moses expressed his worry about his slow speech.[14] God's reply to him has thundered through my mind a hundred times. "Who has made man's mouth? Or who makes the mute, the deaf, the seeing, or the blind? Have not I, the Lord?"[15]

Didn't the Lord make me? It was easy for God to heal me. Prevailing beliefs of physicians, theologians, or other Christians had nothing to do with it.

I noticed that even after God sent ten plagues upon Egypt and delivered the children of Israel from all of them, bringing them out of bondage with all of Egypt's wealth, His people still doubted Him and feared destruction as they camped beside the Red Sea. The words, provided by God through His faithful servant, Moses, are like a standard before me: "Do not be afraid. Stand still, and see the salvation of the Lord, which He will accomplish for you today."[16]

When a laboratory test looked worrisome or a doctor told me of incurable disease, I would remember that no situation ever looked more hopeless than when Pharaoh's armies were descending on the children of Israel on one side while escape was blocked by the sea on the other. At those times, when I was alone with my thoughts concerning my condition, I would almost shout, "God says, 'I *am* the Lord; I do not change.'"[17]

My journey of faith in God's healing has not been easy—it has been tough, and it has required diligence. But my God has been faithful to His promises, which do not change.[18]

✤ ✤ ✤

CHAPTER 16

DIANE'S REFLECTIONS

*"My God sent His Angel and shut the lions' mouths,
so that they have not hurt me…"*
—Daniel 6:22a

My husband, Dan Gordeuk, asked me to contribute my perspectives on all that happened to him during his illness and miraculous recovery, telling me that it wasn't just his story, but mine and our son, David's, as well. Dan has done a marvelous work in describing his healing. Here, at his request, then, is his story as David and I experienced it.

It was January 28, 1996. We were celebrating David's second birthday with dinner and an angel food cake with strawberries and whipped cream when Dan's brother Vic called to discuss the reasons Dan should enter the race for a congressional seat and represent Pennsylvania in Washington. I was exasperated. My mother had recently moved into our home, having entered some frightening stages of metastatic melanoma that had originated in her eye. Although my sister took her home with her every evening and my brother met her needs every weekend in her own home, caring for her was nevertheless draining. At the same time, David was a very active toddler, investigating everything, and Dan's surgical practice

Reach Out—Touch Him

kept him away from home much of each day and many nights, as well. As I considered all of this, the thought of Dan's entering politics seemed overwhelming.

And it was! The phone, we soon discovered, consumes much of a candidate's time. Sometimes Dan would hang up and confide that his desk chair was causing him back pain—or maybe it was sitting in the car on all those long drives to political dinners that was stressing his spine. He had also developed a cough that just would not go away. But concerning these symptoms, he complained to no one but me.

The day before the election, my mother passed away. By the time all the ballots were counted two days later, Dan had garnered a very respectable second place in the race for the congressional seat. And I was tired.

Following my mother's funeral, when things quieted down, Dan said, "Let's go to Canada, fishing."

I would have preferred a different respite, but the previous summer, Dan had been caring for his father, who suffered from advanced Parkinson's disease, and he hadn't had the chance to get away to one of his favorite fishing spots—so what could I say?

Because of Dan's back pain, I had to drive, trailing our boat and tending to David, for most of the trip.

"If I could just recline in the passenger seat," Dan told me, "maybe I could get some relief." The pain in his back, which the doctor attributed to irritation of the sciatic nerve, had worsened, and he was coughing regularly.

The weather in Canada was rough, and I refused to take David out on the choppy water. But Dan had come to fish, and so he did. He wore himself out, fighting the elements and catching no fish, and I drove our weary crew back to Pennsylvania.

I must have felt considerable resentment toward being tossed around by all of these circumstances because, on returning, I sensed the surfacing of it in a vow to potty-train David "no matter what someone else might want me to do." Ten days and a half-bag of marshmallows later, I reached my selfish goal, and our boy moved into a new stage of his development. I didn't know then the influence that other aspects of David's growth would have on my own maturation in a time of crisis.

Even at age two, David was a sponge for information. Believing our main obligation was to lead him to the Lord, and wanting to fill his mind with God's teachings, we provided Bible-story tapes and books galore. He learned many of these stories by heart and could recite verses as difficult for his age as John 3:16. Our new goal was to find a church that pleased both Dan and me, one that had a teaching program for two-year-olds. So we spent the summer "church shopping."

I say "we" but, in fact, Dan struggled to be a part of our probe, often finding that he could not manage it. On arrival at the service we had chosen, he'd say, "I'll lie here on the car seat for a while," or he'd leave partway through the service, whispering to me that the pews were aggravating his back pain.

Dan's family reunion was held that summer in the Midwest. Having decided we needed to vacation on our way, we took our camper. I didn't feel comfortable handling so large a vehicle, so Dan was forced to do all the driving—which meant that at each place we chose to stop and sight-see, he could only lie down, hoping to find relief from his pain. The next day would find him sitting miserably in the driver's seat again.

Finally, on arriving at the reunion, Dan assumed the charade of acting normal and gregarious but returned to our room when he could, to lie flat, try the exercises the orthopedic doctor thought might lend relief, or stand in the shower in the hope that moist heat would help. At this point I told him that I didn't want to hear another complaint until he went again to see a doctor. This seemed only to send him into silent suffering.

Reach Out—Touch Him

Back home again, Dan began what became a routine for the coming months: he went to work, seeing patients in his office, the operating room or the emergency room, then returned home to collapse into bed, with intermittent trips to the shower or tub to use up all available hot water in a quest for relief. At night he took up wandering, because lying in bed was so painful. He would go for long walks, come back to shower, and try to sneak in enough sleep to be able to function the next day.

During this time when Dan was almost totally absorbed in trying to gain relief from pain, David wanted to wrestle and "play rough." It hurt Dan so much to have his body jarred in the slightest that I soon became the rough-house partner instead, telling David that Daddy needed to rest.

I was becoming both mommy and daddy to David. Soon Dan wouldn't even join us for dinner; it was too painful for him to sit at the table. He would stand or kneel to eat, then immediately go back to lie down or shower.

With autumn came the season for hunting in Pennsylvania, a time of year and a pastime Dan had customarily loved. The first day of buck season had always meant high excitement to him, but this day was different. He got dressed and walked across our field to his tree stand, then turned around and retraced his steps. He was back in bed, exhausted and hurting, before daylight ever broke.

Dan's father and his caregiver came to our house for Thanksgiving week. Ordinarily, Dan would take over for the caregiver, providing her some time off, but now, he could hardly manage. We were slated to take care of Dad for several weeks around Christmas as well, but I could see that this time it would be impossible.

It wasn't until two weeks into December that Dan's brother Vic, an oncology specialist, came to Pennsylvania for a visit, observed Dan's condition, talked with him, and sent him to the hospital for a complete blood work-up.

Diane's Reflections

Dan's diagnosis, although efficiently handled, required all day and two trips to the emergency room. It was not until the internal medical doctor called me into a private room to explain it to me that I realized it was serious and life threatening. Dan's back pain, this "lion" that had gnawed at our family life for weeks, now appeared ready to devour it altogether, because it was not sciatic nerve pain after all. Prostate cancer had been the culprit for many months prior to this day, and we'd had no suspicion of it.

At home, Dan and I cried together. Maybe, at that point, he comprehended the urgency and finality of his situation better than I. I had not yet reached the depth of understanding that he, as a surgeon, had.

On the following Sunday afternoon, several men from the church came to pray with us. I had been used to praying "politely" for others—for changed hearts, encouragement, and favorable responses to medical treatment. But theirs was a bold prayer, asking primarily that the cancer tumor and pain would leave.

At the prayer's conclusion, Dan jumped off the couch. I smiled—again, politely—and thought, *How nice to see such a positive attitude.*

But that "attitude" didn't change over the next few days. I'd see Dan swinging his arms or bending at the waist, and he'd say, "Diane, the pain is gone!"

The phone rang every five minutes. Its ringing was a nuisance, but the messages were a definite aid to my stability in the face of Dan's illness. Offers of help with any and every need were reassuring. I hung up the receiver many times tearfully thanking God for such good friends. Especially humbling were the hundreds of promises to remember Dan in prayer, and a surprising number of them had a common thread of healing. I remember a call from a sweet lady who promised she'd be "praying and fasting for Dan's healing." It came just before Christmas, and I thought, *Now, there's a gal who*

Reach Out—Touch Him

wants to lose weight before the holidays. I had no clue as to the power of fasting and prayer rendered up to the Lord.

Yet not every call was helpful. One came from a world-renowned cancer research specialist. He identified himself, and I replied, "Oh, yes, you're the doctor who's going to give us some good news."

His tone was somber. "I'm sorry, ma'am. There is no good news for your husband."

We sought the opinion of a different cancer specialist, the most reputable we could find, in New York. I had brought lots of Bible read-along books and tapes to occupy David while Dan and I listened to this doctor's dismal review of "the facts." In front of the X-ray viewing board, he explained that Dan didn't have long to live, and that the medicines they could try were only experimental, with no guaranteed results and terrifically bad side effects.

The lion—this cancer—had us in the pit, and we, like Daniel in the Bible, were being forced to look at it face to face. Because I couldn't run and scream, I wandered to the X-ray board and tried to ask a light but pertinent question. "What do these scans mean?"

The doctor answered, "The bones that appear black on the scans are the ones involved with cancer."

"But they're all black!" I said.

"That's right, ma'am."

I've never been punched in the stomach, but at that moment I knew the feeling. The imminence of my husband's death was clear. I couldn't swallow or speak. When Dan said he would take the experimental treatment offered, I was only able to nod in agreement.

On the way home, I asked Dan about his back pain. It was still absent, no matter what the finest doctor in the country had to tell us. God had given us a mighty sign to hold in our hearts.

Diane's Reflections

From childhood, I'd been immersed in church music. It was almost as if God had led me to store away all His promises in song for this very crisis. Over and over the words rolled through my head:

> "Safe in the arms of Jesus…"[1]
> "His eye is on the sparrow, and I know he watches me…"[2]
> "All I have needed Thy hand hath provided…"[3]
> "And he walks with me, and he talks with me…"[4]
> "What a friend we have in Jesus…"[5]
> "There is a place of quiet rest, near to the heart of God…"[6]
> …and so many more….

I've mentioned our son David's spiritual growth and its effect on my own. It began one day when David came to me in tears, telling me he didn't know how he could believe the Bible was real. "It seems like the other stories you read to me that are make-believe." His struggle brought wetness to my own eyes.

"David," I said, gathering him into my arms, "don't worry. It will all come. If you keep learning, you'll go through life putting your trust in God. He'll prove Himself real to you, and one day you'll be able to look back and see where and how He was faithful. Then you'll know—the Bible is real."

As he ran off to play, I thanked God for reminding me that it really is as simple as that. Childlike faith. Faith as small as a mustard seed. I thought of one of the stories we had read often to David, the one I mentioned above, about Daniel in the lion's den. Was it make-believe? A man in a den all night with lions that lay peacefully in the opposite corner?

No, Daniel was a real man who got dressed each morning and went to work and who sat down at mid-day to eat with colleagues. And the lions in the dungeon den were real—man-eaters that tore flesh and crushed bones with their teeth. Their job was to eat people!

Reach Out—Touch Him

Daniel would have realized that. Was he afraid? Did he tremble and cry? Did he wonder how the Lord could ever protect him from such ravenous appetites, such powerful jaws?

Was it a children's story? No, it was a story for me. Because my husband Dan's cancer was real and it could devour him, God gave me a glimpse of what the biblical Daniel's thoughts could have been as he faced death in the den. And over the next few weeks, He sent my husband and me the same comfort he must have sent to the prophet Daniel as, increasingly, through the long, dark night of clinging to our God, we put our trust, our weakness, our very lives into His hands. What soaring joy awaited both the prophet and us when, "in the morning," we found Him faithful!

Dan's miracle occurred as believers bombarded the gates of heaven with bold and selfless prayers, in childlike faith. He has shared this account so that you may believe and, when in need of healing, may find it the way he did. His story is one of faith and victory, and I am blessed to be both his wife and his witness to the fact. May God be praised!

It is not up to man to prove God's promises. God made the promises, and He will prove Himself. Blessed be the name of the Lord.

❦ ❦ ❦

EPILOGUE

MEDICINES, MEDICAL TREATMENT, AND HEALING WITHOUT USE OF THEM

This book records my journey of faith and gives a chronology of God's marvelous miracle of healing my body. As I mentioned early in the account, I felt impressed by God to do all that I could do, trusting that He would do the rest. Additionally, Diane and I felt that good stewardship, as taught in God's Word, included my acceptance of all that the field of medicine had to offer. In retrospect, however, I believe that some of the medication I was given was damaging rather than helpful and that, during the times when I was taking these medications, God protected me from their harmful effects.

To complete the account of my healing, I would like to mention all the forms of medical treatment that were given to me.

First, I received chemotherapy in the form of six Cisplatin, or Cis-platinum, injections, one each month for six months. At the same time, I was given two hormonally active drugs by mouth. Then I was put on hormone-blocking agents, which I have continued until the writing of this book. I also received a vaccine against prostate cancer that is designed to build immunity in the same way that a vaccine against tetanus works to help the body resist that disease.

Reach Out—Touch Him

Last, almost two years after I was healed, when there was no trace of prostate cancer in my body, the doctors decided that, because they had never treated my prostate gland, they should implant radon seeds in it.[1] Their reasoning was that, until this time, I was being treated as if I were incurable, but now it seemed evident that I was cured, and it would be wise, under the circumstances, to treat the prostate gland so that another cancer would not occur there.

I know that there are people who believe that any kind of medical treatment is inappropriate, at best, and shows a lack of faith, at worst. I do not take issue with anyone who believes this way. I do, however, note that if I had not gone back to the doctors at regular intervals, there would be no medical documentation of my healing, and my testimony would be less credible.

It seems to me ludicrous that those treatments which the doctors all declared to be ineffective in patients of my age group are now brought forth by some as the reason for my sound health, when it is, instead, the result of the healing power of Almighty God, to Whom we owe all glory and praise. This book, therefore, records my testimony to the fact that I was not healed by medications or, indeed, by any medical means but, rather, by God's grace and power, in the name of Jesus.

AFTERWORD

For nine full years after his miraculous victory over terminal cancer, Dr. Daniel Gordeuk lived a healthy and vigorous life, making himself available to hundreds of people seeking his guidance in their own quests for healing. This book records not only his recovery of wellness but the resources that sustained him prior to and following that day in December, 1996, when the miracle occurred.

ACKNOWLEGMENTS

This book could not have been developed or published without the contributions of a number of specialists:

Working from Dan's hand-written text and a draft typed by Denise Hessler, Laurel West edited and refined the manuscript and moved it toward publication.

Elaine Stedelbauer of Green Frog Design combined our back-cover copy with images she selected and skillfully enhanced to create the cover we desired. Dick Brown reproduced his original, fine photo of Dan in extraordinarily high resolution for the back cover.

My son, David, and I are grateful for the services of each of these courteous and efficient professionals. At the same time, we recognize that there would have been no story to tell if God had not done His miraculous work of healing in Dan's body. To Him we offer not only our humble thanks but praise and glory, as well.

Diane J. Gordeuk

END NOTES

Preface

1. Malachi 3:6a

Chapter 1

1. John 12:32. "And I, if I am lifted up from the earth, will draw all peoples to Myself."
2. I John 1:9. If we confess our sins, He is faithful and just to forgive us our sins and to cleanse us from all unrighteousness.

Chapter 2

1. Matthew 6:33. "But seek first the kingdom of God and His righteousness, and all these things shall be added to you."
2. II Corinthians 12:9
3. Psalm 71:2. Deliver me in Your righteousness, and cause me to escape; [i]ncline Your ear to me, and save me.

Chapter 3

1. A narcotic used to stop pain, somewhat stronger than codeine
2. *Metastatic* means the cancer has spread to other organs.
3. A blood test to check men for prostate cancer

4. Rectal examination
5. Having a low red blood cell count
6. Red blood cells are produced in the bone marrow.
7. See Acts 9:10; 10:3; 10:9-13; and16:9, 10.

Chapter 5

1. The Christian Broadcasting Network
2. See II Kings, Chapter 5.

Chapter 6

1. See Luke 12:41-48; Matthew 25:14-30.
2. See passage at the head of this chapter.
3. II Kings, Chapter 5
4. John 9:6, 7
5. Psalm 22:3. But You are holy, [e]nthroned in the praises of Israel.
6. Acts 1:8a. "But you shall receive power when the Holy Spirit has come upon you."

Chapter 7

1. Matthew 7:9-11
2. John 15:13. "Greater love has no one than this, than to lay down one's life for his friends."
3. Malachi 3:6a
4. Psalm 105:8
5. Isaiah 55:8, 9. "For My thoughts are not your thoughts, [n]or are your ways My ways," says the Lord. "For as the heavens are higher than the earth, [s]o are My ways higher than your ways, [a]nd My thoughts than your thoughts."

6. Luke 18:27

7. Romans 1:16. For I am not ashamed of the gospel of Christ, for it is the power of God to salvation for everyone who believes, for the Jew first and also for the Greek.

8. Matthew 18:2b-4. "Assuredly, I say to you, unless you are converted and become as little children, you will in no wise enter the kingdom of heaven. Therefore whoever humbles himself as this little child is the greatest in the kingdom of heaven."

9. I Samuel 16:7c. "For the Lord does not see as man sees; for man looks at the outward appearance, but the Lord looks at the heart."

10. Hebrews 13:8

11. Mark 6:3-5

12. Matthew 9:2b, 3. When Jesus saw their faith, He said to the paralytic, "Son, be of good cheer; your sins are forgiven you." And at once some of the scribes said within themselves, "This man blasphemes."

13. *The Physician's Desk Reference*

14. See Isaiah 55:8, 9

15. Luke 13:11, 12, 16. And behold, there was a woman who had a spirit of infirmity eighteen years, and was bent over and could in no way raise herself up. But when Jesus saw her, He called her to Him and said to her, "Woman, you are loosed from your infirmity."

16. Matthew 8:16b, 17. And He…healed all who were sick, that it might be fulfilled which was spoken by Isaiah the prophet, saying: "He Himself took our infirmities [a]nd bore our sicknesses."

17. Psalm 119:90a

Chapter 8

1. Exodus 4:10b, 12
2. Ephesians 3:20

Chapter 9

1. Genesis 12:1
2. Genesis 12:4a
3. Genesis 18:10b
4. Genesis 18:13, 14a
5. Genesis 15:5
6. Genesis 22:2
7. Genesis 22:3a
8. Acts 10:34. Then Peter…said: "In truth I perceive that God shows no partiality."
9. Matthew 8:13. Then Jesus said to the centurion, "Go your way; and as you have believed, so let it be done for you." And his servant was healed that same hour.
10. Luke 22:31, 32a
11. I Corinthians 2:14. But the natural man does not receive the things of the Spirit of God, for they are foolishness to him; nor can he know them, because they are spiritually discerned.
12. See Chapter 10.
13. Acts 4:29, 30
14. See Matthew 9:21, 22.

Chapter 10

1. John 14:18a
2. John 14:26; 16:13. "But the Helper, the Holy Spirit, whom the Father will send in My name, He will teach you all things, and bring to your remembrance all things that I said to you. …[W]hen He, the Spirit of truth has come, He will guide you into all truth…"
3. Acts 1:4
4. Acts 1:8a
5. Acts 2:2-4

END NOTES

6. I Corinthians 6:19. Or do you not know that your body is the temple of the Holy Spirit who is in you, whom you have from God, and you are not your own?
7. Psalm 50:15b. "I will deliver you, and you shall glorify Me."
8. John 5:14. Afterward Jesus found him in the temple, and said to him, "See, you have been made well. Sin no more, lest a worse thing come upon you."
9. Acts 8:26-40
10. Acts 10:34
11. I Samuel 3:1-10
12. I Samuel 3:1b
13. Acts 4:29
14. Isaiah 6:8b

Chapter 11

1. An anticancer drug
2. Luke 18:27
3. See Chapter 3.
4. Acts 3:6
5. Acts 4:29

Chapter 12

1. Genesis 18:9-15
2. Genesis 22:1, 2
3. Genesis 22:9-19

Chapter 13

1. Matthew 16:19. "And I will give you the keys of the kingdom of heaven, and whatever you loose on earth will be loosed in heaven."

2. Isaiah 53:5, concerning peace: But He was wounded for our transgressions, He was bruised for our iniquities; [t]he chastisement for our peace was upon Him, [a]nd by His stripes we are healed.
3. John 3:7, 8. "Do not marvel that I said to you, You must be born again.' The wind blows where it wishes, and you hear the sound of it, but cannot tell where it comes from and where it goes. So is everyone who is born of the Spirit."
4. See Acts 4:29

Chapter 14

1. John 14:26. "But the Helper, the Holy Spirit, whom the Father will send in My name, He will teach you all things...."
2. I John 1:9. If we confess our sins, He is faithful and just to forgive us our sins and to cleanse us from all unrighteousness.
3. James 5:16. Confess your trespasses to one another, and pray for one another, that you may be healed.
4. James 5:14, 15. Is anyone among you sick? Let him call for the elders of the church, and let them pray over him, anointing him with oil in the name of the Lord. And the prayer of faith will save the sick, and the Lord will raise him up. And if he has committed sins, he will be forgiven. Also, I John 1:9. If we confess our sins, He is faithful and just to forgive us our sins and to cleanse us from all unrighteousness.
5. Psalm 50:15. "Call upon Me in the day of trouble; I will deliver you, and you shall glorify Me."
6. John 14:26 (See End Note 1.)
7. Luke 22:31, 32. And the Lord said, "Simon, Simon! Indeed, Satan has asked for you, that he may sift you as wheat. But I have prayed

for you that your faith should not fail; and when you have returned to Me, strengthen your brethren."

8. Matthew 17:20b. "…for assuredly, I say to you, if you have faith as a mustard seed, you will say to this mountain, 'Move from here to there,' and it will move; and nothing will be impossible for you."

9. See Acts, Chapter 2.

10. John 5:14. Afterward Jesus found him in the temple, and said to him, "See, you have been made well. Sin no more, lest a worse thing come upon you."

11. Isaiah 45:18, 19. "…I am the Lord, and there is no other. …I did not say to the seed of Jacob, 'Seek Me in vain'…"

Chapter 15

1. Isaiah 26:3a
2. Luke 22:31, 32a
3. Acts 10:34
4. Isaiah 53:5
5. I Corinthians 6:19, 20. Or do you not know that your body is the temple of the Holy Spirit who is in you, whom you have from God, and you are not your own? For you were bought at a price; therefore glorify God in your body and in your spirit, which are God's.
6. I Corinthians 6:19, 20; Psalm 50:15
7. Romans 10:11. For the Scripture says, "Whoever believes on Him will not be put to shame."
8. Genesis 12:4a. So Abram departed as the Lord had spoken to him….
9. Genesis 15:1. After these things, the word of the Lord came to Abram in a vision, saying, "Do not be afraid, Abram. I am your shield, your exceedingly great reward."
10. Genesis 15:6
11. Exodus 3:2a

12. Exodus 3:5b
13. Exodus 3:14a
14. Exodus 4:10
15. Exodus 4:11
16. Exodus 14:13a
17. Malachi 3:6a
18. Psalm 105:8. He remembers His covenant forever, [t]he word which He commanded, for a thousand generations.

Chapter 16

1. "Safe in the arms of Jesus," *From the hymn titled the same. Text: Fanny Crosby; Music: W. Howard Doane, 1868, MIDI score.*
2. "His eye is on the sparrow, and I know he watches me," *His Eye is on the Sparrow. Text: Civilla D. Martin; Music: Charles H. Gabriel.*
3. "All I have needed Thy hand hath provided," *Great is Thy Faithfulness. Text: Thomas O. Chisolm; Music: William M. Runyan,* © Hope Publishing Co. Used by permission.
4. "And he walks with me, and he talks with me," *In the Garden. Text and music: C. Austin Miles.*
5. "What a friend we have in Jesus" *Text: Joseph M. Scriven*
6. "There is a place of quiet rest, near to the heart of God," *Near to the Heart of God. Text and music: Cleland B. McAfee.*

Epilogue

1. An outpatient procedure taking forty minutes

CPSIA information can be obtained at www.ICGtesting.com
Printed in the USA
LVOW01s1610011113
359628LV00031B/1153/P